EXPONENTIAL ORGANIZATIONS IN ACTION

Community-Curated Case Studies Transforming An Abundant Future

Authors:

Niki Faldemolaei, Doug Gray PhD, Michael Friebe PhD, Connie Rascon-Gunther, Greg Apodaca, Jonathan Frost, Christine McDougall, Huba Rostonics, Fabrizio Gramuglio, Stacey Murphy, Hans Smith, Rob Bassani

DISCLAIMER

The opinions, analyses, and case studies presented in this book are based on information available as of Aug 2024 and are intended for informational and educational purposes only. They do not constitute financial, legal, or investment advice. The authors are independent contributors, and their views do not necessarily reflect those of other authors, editors, or Temple Arts Publishing.

Readers should conduct their own research and consult qualified professionals before making decisions based on this information. The authors and Temple Arts Publishing disclaim any liability for actions taken or not taken based on the book's content.

COPYRIGHT © 2024 BY THE RESPECTIVE AUTHORS

This work is licensed under the Creative Commons Attribution-NonCommercial-ShareAlike 4.0 International License (CC BY-NC-SA 4.0), with the following additional permission:

Educational Use Exemption: Notwithstanding the non-commercial restriction, this work may be used, adapted, and shared in educational courses and training programs, including those for which tuition or fees are charged, provided that:

1. The use is primarily for instructional purposes.
2. Proper attribution is given.
3. Any adaptations are shared under the same license terms.

eBook ISBN: 978-0-9908165-3-9
Paperback ISBN: 978-0-9908165-4-6
Published by Temple Arts Publishing USA

FOREWORD

When we first introduced the concept of Exponential Organizations (ExOs) in 2014, we knew we were onto something transformative. What we couldn't have predicted was how quickly and profoundly this framework would be adopted across industries and around the globe. The book you hold in your hands is a testament to that journey and, more importantly, a beacon lighting the way forward.

As the founder and chairman of OpenExO and the founding executive director of Singularity University, I've had the privilege of witnessing firsthand how exponential thinking can revolutionize businesses and solve complex global challenges. But what truly excites me about "Exponential Organizations in Action" is that it's not just another business book – it's a community-curated manifesto for a new way of operating in our rapidly changing world.

The case studies within these pages represent more than just success stories. They embody the spirit of exponential growth, demonstrating how organizations of all sizes can leverage emerging technologies, tap into the power of crowds, and create scalable solutions that address our world's most pressing issues. From reimagining healthcare delivery to revolutionizing sustainable architecture, these stories prove that the ExO methodology is not just theoretical – it's a practical, powerful tool for creating abundance.

What sets this book apart is its grassroots origin. It's not a top-down prescription but a bottom-up revolution, curated by the very community that's living and breathing these principles every day. This collaborative approach mirrors the ExO attributes we've long advocated for, and it's heartening to see it in action.

As a future civilization strategist, I'm acutely aware of the challenges we face as a species. Climate change, wealth inequality, and technological disruption are just a few of the complex issues demanding our attention. But after reading these case studies, I'm more optimistic than ever. The exponential leaders featured here are not waiting for solutions – they're creating them, and in doing so, they're shaping a future of abundance for all.

To the reader, I offer both a challenge and an invitation. The challenge is to look beyond the stories and see yourself as part of this exponential revolution. The invitation is to join our growing community of exponential thinkers and doers. Whether you're an entrepreneur, a corporate leader, a policymaker, or simply someone who cares about our collective future, there's a place for you in this movement.

The future is not something that happens to us – it's something we create. With the ExO framework as our guide and the inspiring examples in this book as our motivation, we have the power to build a world of abundance, sustainability, and shared prosperity.

In the recent words of Marc Andreessen, "Let's Build... but build Exponentially!"

Salim Ismail
Founder and Chairman, OpenExO
Founding Executive Director, Singularity University
Future of Civilization Strategist

TABLE OF CONTENTS

Chapter 1: *Exponential Communities - Catalyzing Change in the Modern World* 7

Chapter 2: *Family Business Consulting* 19

Chapter 3: *Future Health Transformation - applying exponential and syntropic principles for the design of a Purpose Investment Fund* 31

Chapter 4: *Becoming Lean and Exponential – when trends impact industries* 47

Chapter 5: *Green Economy Evolution: From Community Conversations to Exponential Action* 59

Chapter 6: *Beyond IQ: Uncovering Hidden Talents - A Future Retrospective* 73

Chapter 7: *SYNTROPIC Enterprise Principles for Dummies — A Primer for a Novel Economic Reasoning and Start-Up Implementation Concepts* 85

Chapter 8: *The ExO Spectrum: From Giants to Nimble Startups (and Everything In-between)* 101

Chapter 9: *Game-Changing the Future of Business* 121

Chapter 10: *Democratizing Finance: Leveraging DeFi in an Organization* 161

Chapter 11: *Regenerative Architecture: Disrupting the $17 Trillion Construction Industry* 177

Chapter 12: *A dualistic presentation of the Immune System* 197

Epilogue: *Igniting the Exponential Awakening* 211

Glossary 213

CHAPTER 1
EXPONENTIAL COMMUNITIES - CATALYZING CHANGE IN THE MODERN WORLD

NIKI FALDEMOLAEI

In the rapidly evolving landscape of the 21st century, we stand at the cusp of a new technological and sustainable revolution. The old ways of doing business and building communities are no longer sufficient to address the complex challenges we face. This book, "Exponential Organizations In Action: Community-Curated Case Studies Transforming An Abundant Future," offers a comprehensive exploration of how businesses and communities can thrive in this era of exponential change.

At the heart of this transformation lies the power of community - not just as beneficiaries of change, but as active catalysts driving innovation and progress. From established eco-villages to emerging decentralized autonomous organizations, communities around the world are embracing exponential technologies and methodologies to create scalable solutions for our most pressing global issues.

The Exponential Organization (ExO) framework, pioneered by Salim Ismail and further developed by a community of innovators, provides a blueprint for leveraging these technologies and methodologies. Three key attributes of ExOs that are particularly relevant to community-building are experimentation, community engagement, and leveraging assets.

Experimentation: The Power of Rapid Iteration

Exponential communities thrive on a culture of constant experimentation. They understand that in a rapidly changing world, the ability to quickly test, learn, and adapt is crucial. This approach is exemplified by initiatives like the 30-Doubling Challenge, where community members experience the exponential curve firsthand. We mastered getting people to persevere to reach the knee of the curve with those last 6 steps paying out massive rewards!

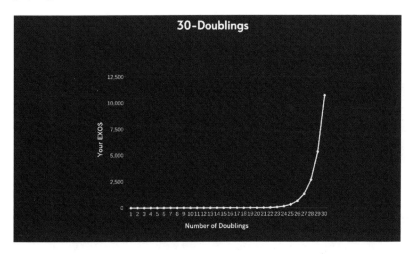

Case Study: The 30-Doubling Challenge

The 30-Doubling Challenge, implemented by the OpenExO community, demonstrates the power of experimentation in driving exponential growth. Participants were tasked with performing a variety of community engagement tasks of mixed choice for 30 doublings. The results were stimulating:

- 70% of participants achieved significant improvements in their engagement results
- On average, participants achieved a 120x improvement over the 30-doublings
- 90% of active participants reported that the challenge changed their perspective on purpose and possibility that comes with applying the ExO attributes

This experiment not only showcased the potential of exponential thinking but also fostered a sense of community as participants shared their experiences and supported each other's growth.

Community Engagement: The Heart of Exponential Growth

Successful exponential communities prioritize deep, meaningful engagement among their members. They create multiple touchpoints for interaction, foster a sense of belonging, and encourage member-led initiatives. The OpenExO Experience is a prime example of how community engagement can drive innovation and growth.

Case Study: The OpenExO Experience

Initially designed as an onboarding tool, the OpenExO Experience evolved into a powerful community engagement education platform:

- Participation grew 5X from Season One to Season Two
- Participants associated ExO attributes with their businesses, leading to over 300 unique case studies referenced in their reporting
- 78% of participants reported implementing at least one new ExO attribute in their organization
- The community-curated case studies culminated in a #1 international bestselling book, showcasing the power of collective intelligence

This initiative not only deepened members' understanding of ExO principles but also created a valuable resource for the wider business community.

Leveraging Assets: Maximizing Resources for Exponential Impact

Exponential communities excel at identifying and leveraging both internal and external assets. This includes not just physical resources, but also knowledge, networks, and emerging technologies. The ExO Angels initiative demonstrates how communities can leverage diverse assets to drive positive change.

Case Study: ExO Angels

ExO Angels, a community-driven initiative, focuses on leveraging the collective assets of its members to support experimental projects:

- Over 100 people supported in year one
- 5 million tokenized resources (time, expertise, connections) mobilized and distributed in 3yr
- 30% of supported projects achieved significant milestones (transformation, innovation awards, successful project funding, etc.), the rest failed forward aka pivoted into more suitable paths
- Create and test unique models of asset-based investing and vector money that goes beyond traditional financial models.

This initiative showcases how communities can amplify their impact by creatively leveraging their collective resources.

The Evolving Role of Community Leadership

As communities become more decentralized and technologically enabled, the role of community leadership is evolving. The job descriptions for the Chief Community Officer, Head of Community and Community Manager provides insight into the skills and mindset required to lead exponential communities:

"As A360/PhDVentures Head of Community, your mission is to enhance the membership experience through immersive and impactful interactions that foster deep connections and deliver unparalleled value. From leading and executing virtual workshops and masterminds to empowering members to organize local meetups, you'll ensure each touchpoint enriches the community experience, ultimately driving member retention, referrals, and the overall growth of the A360 community."

This description emphasizes the need for leaders who can:
1. Design and execute transformative engagement strategies
2. Empower member-led initiatives
3. Leverage technology for enhanced community interaction
4. Foster deep connections among target demographics
5. Align community activities with the organization's mission and values

Additional candidate credentials further illustrate the diverse experiences that can contribute to effective community leadership in an exponential context:

- Experience running retreat centers, facilitating transformational workshops, un-conferences and swarms
- Implementation of engagement initiatives like gamification and reward challenges
- Expertise in relationship management with high-net-worth individuals and family offices
- Integration of emerging technologies, from digital publishing to blockchain and AI
- Alignment with exponential thinking through involvement with organizations like Singularity University, XPrize and OpenExO
- Cross promotions in joint projects like Exponential Organizations V2.0 (a book curated by the community and authored by Salim Ismail and Peter Diamandis)

These examples highlight the multifaceted nature of community leadership in the exponential age, combining traditional community-building skills with technological savvy and a deep understanding of exponential principles.

Emerging Trends in Exponential Communities

As we look to the future, several trends are shaping the evolution of exponential communities:

Exponential Organizations in Action

1. AI-Driven Engagement: Communities are increasingly leveraging AI tools to enhance member interactions, provide personalized experiences, and generate insights. For example, the use of AI bots in launching the Exponential Organizations V2.0 book demonstrates the potential of AI in community-driven content creation.

2. Decentralized Governance: Blockchain technology is enabling new models of community governance, as seen in the rise of Decentralized Autonomous Organizations (DAOs). These structures allow for more transparent, participatory decision-making processes. See case studies covering Lido, Maker DAO and Rocket Pool in chapter 10 and ReFi DAO here in Chapter 1.

3. Immersive Experiences: The integration of virtual and augmented reality technologies create new possibilities for community engagement, particularly in remote or distributed communities. Un-conferences & swarms are examples of high-level interactive working sessions that commonly take place online with mixed media resources available in web3 platforms. SciFiHive.com

4. Purpose-Driven Initiatives: Communities are increasingly organizing around shared purposes, particularly in addressing global challenges. The focus on SDG compliance and green economy initiatives within the ExO communities exemplify this trend. See Community 3.0^x in chapter 5.

5. Cross-Pollination of Ideas: Exponential communities are breaking down traditional silos, encouraging the exchange of ideas across different sectors and disciplines. This cross-pollination is driving innovation and creating unexpected solutions to complex problems. ExI, ExO Angels, Purpose Alliance, wgAI have all engaged in cross-project initiatives.

6. The Sophia Century: Named after the Greek word for wisdom, represents a paradigm shift in how we approach global challenges. It is an era where collective intelligence, empathy and exponential thinking converge to create transformative solutions. At the heart of this new approach is the reimagining of how we gather, share knowledge, and catalyze action. See Chapter 5 and the book Empathy in Action by Tony Bates and Natalie Petouhoff.

Case Studies of Transformative Communities

To further illustrate the power of exponential communities, let's examine a few case studies of both established and emerging initiatives:

1. Findhorn Ecovillage (Scotland)

Established in 1962, Findhorn has become a globally recognized model for sustainable living:

- Reduced ecological footprint to about half the UK average
- Generates 100% of its electricity from renewable sources
- Hosts thousands of visitors annually at its education center despite a triad of recent setbacks

Key Lesson: The importance of integrating social, economic, and environmental sustainability in community design.

2. ReFi DAO (Decentralized Autonomous Organization) (Portugal)

A rapidly growing community focused on regenerative finance:

- Successfully launched multiple projects promoting sustainable economic practices
- Leveraged blockchain technology for transparent, community-driven governance

Key Lesson: The potential of aligning financial incentives with environmental goals through decentralized collaboration.

3. Burning Man (USA)

Grown from a small gathering to a global cultural movement:
- Created a unique model of temporary community based on radical self-reliance and expression
- Spawned numerous spin-off communities and year-round initiatives (check out Gathering of Tribes)

Key Lesson: The power of participatory culture in building transformative communities, even in temporary settings.

4. Big Blue Sky (Australia)

An initiative that modeled syntropic principles (see chapter 7) based on Buckminster Fuller's work:
- Generated 14 moonshots for the future of the city Gold Coast
- Addressed culture, carbon footprint, economic resilience, and more

Key Lesson: The potential for synergistic collaboration between diverse stakeholders in creating bold visions for the future.

5. Damanhur (Italy)

Developed a complex society with its own constitution, currency, and schools.
- Created impressive artistic and architectural achievements (e.g., underground temples).
- Pioneered research in alternative healing and eco-technology

Key Lesson: Demonstrated potential for communities to become centers of innovation and creativity.

Lessons on what not to do (derived from various community failures):

1. Avoid over-dependence on charismatic leaders.
2. Ensure transparent and inclusive decision-making processes.
3. Balance idealism with practical and sustainable economic models.
4. Avoid isolation from the broader society; maintain positive external relationships.
5. Establish clear conflict resolution mechanisms.
6. Avoid rigid ideological positions that may alienate members or hinder adaptation.
7. Ensure diversity and prevent the formation of exclusive in-groups.
8. Maintain a balance between community goals and individual needs/freedoms.

New communities watch list, aka hopeful launches with fresh eyes:

New Earth Ecosystem / NeosLife (Portugal), Gaianet (Netherlands), Lake Nona FL (Fountain Life Headquarters), Futurville's Vulcanville Canada (Live Long and Prosper)

These case studies demonstrate the diverse ways in which communities can leverage exponential thinking and technologies to drive positive change. They highlight the importance of shared values, innovative governance models, and the integration of sustainability principles in community design.

Conclusion: The Path Forward

As we navigate the complexities of the 21st century, exponential communities offer a powerful model for driving positive change. By embracing experimentation, fostering deep engagement, and creatively leveraging assets, these communities are creating scalable solutions to some of our most pressing global challenges.

The examples and case studies presented in this chapter are just the beginning. As you explore the pages that follow, you'll discover a wealth of insights, strategies, and inspiration for building and nurturing exponential communities. Whether you're a business leader, a community organizer, or simply an individual passionate about creating positive change, the principles outlined in this book offer a roadmap for harnessing the power of community in the exponential age.

We invite you to see yourself not just as a reader, but as an active participant in this global movement of exponential communities. The challenges we face are significant, but so too is our collective potential to create solutions. By embracing exponential thinking and the power of community, we can build a future of abundance, sustainability, and shared prosperity.

As we embark on this journey together, remember that the future is not something that happens to us - it's something we create together. Welcome to the world of Exponential Organizations in Action. The transformation starts now, and it starts with you.

Contact the Author:

Niki Faldemolaei has been building and serving communities since childhood. Born to entrepreneurial parents she grew up amidst a snow ski resort in winters and fishing resort in summers followed by her own venture into running transformational communities in Sedona AZ and Hawaii where she experimented with off grid living. An avid early adopter she studied biotechnology at university and returned to the future of exponential technologies when 20 Gutenberg moments were about to be disrupted. This book is a compilation of the awakening that science and metaphysics are now accepted as our origins and becoming mainstream.

Co-Founder, Board Advisor, new CEO; Community Experience Officer
http://exoangels.com
https://www.linkedin.com/in/faldemolaei

CHAPTER 2
FAMILY BUSINESS CONSULTING

DOUG GRAY PHD

We are currently experiencing the largest transfer of wealth in human history-- over $74 trillion. Family business leaders on Main Streets and home offices-- not on Wall Street-- drive most of the economy, Gross Domestic Product (GDP), and job creation in every community. Throughout history. In every corner of the world. Common examples range from agriculture to finance, from manufacturing to retail, from construction to real estate.

Family business leaders in the United States, for instance, drive over 65% of the gross domestic product (GDP) and over 70% of new jobs. Over 95% of businesses are closely held by private owners. Those percentages are even higher in Europe and Asia. Too many small businesses are being acquired by private equity investors or large publicly traded companies.

The consulting sector typically focuses on specialized expertise, such as wealth, legal, or asset management. A more comprehensive approach, called Family Business Consulting, focuses on the process dynamics for governance, succession, continuity, and legacy. Although family businesses are the social fabric of global exponential change, most family business leaders hesitate to invest in consulting. They don't know how to assess the capacity of their next (rising) generation.

Older family business leaders say, "I can't sleep. I don't know who is capable of taking over my business. And frankly, I don't know what else I'd do."

Younger family business leaders say, "I'm stuck in the middle. Our people think I'm in charge, but I still need to get approvals from my father or the owners."

Older family business leaders need to give up control and develop their multi-generational purpose or legacy. But they don't know how to do so.

Younger family business leaders need to practice new behaviors, to gain clarity about succession and ownership steps. They don't know how to do so.

Problem

The consulting sector typically focuses on specialized expertise, such as wealth, legal, or asset management. A more comprehensive approach, called Family Business Consulting, focuses on the process dynamics for governance, succession, continuity, and legacy. Although family businesses are the social fabric of global exponential change, most family business leaders hesitate to invest in consulting.

The problem is that most family business leaders are confused. The older generation owners don't know how to assess the capabilities of potential successors. The younger Next Generation leaders don't know how to demonstrate their capacity. They all need more career clarity and less conflict. They need to sleep better at night. They need both 1) an effective process and 2) validated content. They need better family business consulting.

Solution

Theoretical models are pictures used to describe problems (See Figure 1.) Our experience is that Family Enterprises are more complex than any other type of business, therefore our theoretical model describes the complex relationships of these 5 systems— the individual, family, business, learning, and ownership systems.

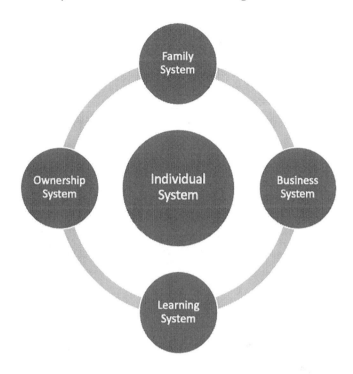

Figure 1. The Assess Next GenTM theoretical model for Family Business leaders

The central questions for every leader include:
How do I fit in?
What is my capability?

Those identity questions are the backbone of every family business, social psychology, and Industrial/Organizational psychology. Those questions also describe how you learned "your place in the world." And those questions describe how your children fit into your family. Each of these five systems is based on our assumptions, and the following lists may be useful for any consultant or leader.

The Individual System is based on these four assumptions:
1. You have agency/ choice.
2. You have the capacity to flourish.
3. Your individual awareness drives your behaviors and career(s).
4. Practicing leadership requires both knowing/awareness and showing/actions

The Family System is based on these assumptions:
1. Your elders have shared values, assumptions, and behaviors that may be stated/ unstated.
2. Your current family will change over time.
3. How you communicate, make decisions, and address conflict can be improved.
4. You need a safe process for assessing and developing the unique strengths of your key leaders.

The Business System is based on these assumptions:
1. Your global, networked market demands will increase in complexity.
2. Your technology-based solutions will define your success.
3. Your working teams are the fundamental units in all successful businesses.
4. Great managers maximize the productivity and profitability of others.

The Learning System is based on these assumptions:
1. Your curiosity is innate and can be nurtured.
2. Practicing personal mastery is the cornerstone of your learning organization.
3. Your mental models are like videos of your potential.
4. Great leaders co-create a shared vision of a better future.

The Ownership System is based on these assumptions:
1. Your core business(es) define your unique competitive advantage(s).
2. Your demand for responsible stewardship is endless and complex.
3. Your talent development system needs accurate, practical data.
4. Continual learning can accelerate your capacity for innovation, resilience, and profitability.

To repeat, the central questions for every leader include:
How do I fit in?
What is my capability?

That complexity requires both a process solution and validated content.

We created Assess Next Gen™ (ANG) in 2022 in response to a perceived market gap between what family business leaders want and what consultants can provide. Doug Gray, PhD, and Kent Rhodes, EdD, met as consultants with The Family Business Consulting Group (FBCG, founded 30 years ago and described at www.theFBCG.com).

We knew that 360 assessments are the most valid performance feedback process known to organizational development psychologists. And we knew that there were no 360 assessments designed to measure the complexity of family business leaders. A 360 is a way for multiple raters, with different perspectives, to share feedback about a colleague's behavior. 360 assessments are now defined by best practices that define rigor, confidentiality, and relevance. For instance, our confidential process includes up to 7 rater groups (owners, board, managers, peers, direct reports, family/friends, and self), quantitative behavioral feedback (strengths, weaknesses, gaps), and qualitative feedback (written and interview data).

Solution Sprints

In 2022 we designed, globally validated, and developed a 360 leadership assessment consultative process for family business leaders, described at www.AssessNextGen.com.

In 2023 we developed over 30 use cases with 7 consultants, and hundreds of raters, in 11 client organizations.

In Q1-Q2 2023, Doug developed a self-rater assessment and a licensing model.

In Q4 2023 we designed and sold three Next Gen Peer Group networks for family and non-family leaders to launch in 2024.

In Q4 2023, using AI to edit the first draft, Doug wrote and published a new product, The Success Playbook for Next-Gen Family Business Leaders

The minimum viable process worked. Now we needed to expand the scope.

ExO Attributes/ Methodology

MTP: Consulting for all Next Gen leaders.

Key performance competencies: agility and scalability.

Staff on Demand: In 2022 we invited 37 consultants from the FBCG to use the ANG process with any of their clients or prospects, Doug developed content and sold licenses to consultants, and curated a mailing list of 1,100 potential consultants.

Community & Crowd: In 2023 Doug published 6 articles in professional associations, led podcasts and LinkedIn live sessions, published weekly articles and interviews, and distributed content to his mailing list 2-3 times/ month.

Artificial Intelligence: Using AI prompts, Doug wrote a 120-page book in 4 weeks, called The Success Playbook for Next Gen Family Business Leaders, to be published in December 2023, and available at all online bookstores in January 2024. AI accelerated that product development process.

Leveraged Assets: In 2022-2023, Doug spoke at 3 professional association conferences, met with 50+ centers of influence (COIs) in wealth advisory, estate planning, family offices, centers at colleges or universities, hosted a monthly session within a professional association, developed digital learning content hosted on a platform for all 50 desired behaviors using our theoretical model of five systems (family, business, individual, learning and ownership systems)

Engagement: Within two months, Doug designed and sold hybrid Next Gen Peer Group networks to launch in January 2024, with 80% of registrants new to consulting, designed for both non-family and family leaders, with 10 virtual sessions and two 24-hour direct event sessions in two different cities in the next 12 months

Interfaces: Doug developed a 38-page process model for consultants and licensees to deliver consistent quality 360 assessments using protocols, email templates, and two PDF reports for the quantitative rater data (scores and gaps) and the qualitative data (written and interview responses), and he recorded instructional videos for consultants, then hosted them on a digital learning platform

Experimentation: Doug designed content and hosted a robust digital learning community for the licensees and Next Gen Peer Group participants to access, adapted the 50-item 360 assessment into a 15-item self-rater assessment to be sold online and used in the peer groups, attracted other FBCG consultants to co-facilitate the Next Gen Peer Group networks in 2024

Autonomy: As independent consultants, with encouragement from our FBCG colleagues, we developed Assess Next GenTM as a separate business, then invested startup funds, and assumed all associated costs and benefits.

Social: Doug wrote weekly digital articles, videos, and podcasts and hired a marketing manager to publish and distribute content on Linked In, two blogs, Facebook ads, Google ads, and articles published weekly on SubStack.

Lessons Learned Include:

Experimentation: We repeatedly practiced the "design-measure-learn" cycle and sought feedback from clients and consultants, developed and shared new processes designed to improve consistency, quality, and profitability. However, we do not have many use cases yet and need more feedback.

Dashboards and OKRs: Not used yet, even though Doug published Objectives + Key Results (OKR) Leadership; How to Apply Silicon Valley's Secret Sauce to Your Career, Team or Organization in 2019.

Interfaces: Not yet a platform, although the capacity for large-scale applications may exist.

Engagement: The Next Gen Peer Group process is designed to accelerate engagement, using confidential networks of like-minded leaders, in non-competing businesses. The hybrid design includes 10 virtual sessions and two 24-hour direct events within 12 months. Two expert consultants facilitate the process by focusing on both content and process. The structure of each session is dynamic, and the topics reflect the five systems in the Assess Next Gen research (family, individual, business, learning, and ownership systems).

Use Cases

Here are two representative case studies, at the individual and team levels

Individual Case Study- Family Focus

Nancy had a new Family Business executive coaching client and wanted to explore the possibility of succession for that NextGen leader. Specifically, she wanted to assess the strengths, weaknesses, blind spots, and hidden talents of that leader, beyond the anecdotal feedback from others, and beyond her self-report. Nancy also wanted to deepen the consulting engagement. She wanted to model how family and non-family members could provide professional feedback to one another. She said, "We needed to increase engagement with family members who had never provided direct feedback to one another. This assessment process increased direct communication, and family harmony, and validated the fact that the leader was in fact more than capable of being their next successor." Nancy was able to provide 50 specific behavioral directions for the leader. She also provided feedback on what the leader needed to "start doing, stop doing, and continue doing." This assessment process evolved into a turning point in the family because they stopped acting like separate silos in the business and started to collaborate directly.

Team Case Study- Next Gen Skills Focus

Doug had worked for 18 months with five mid-management leaders in a fast-growing financial services company. They were preparing for a year of transition, with the President and CFO moving into newly created board roles. The owner and executive leadership team requested that this 360-leadership development assessment process be completed within two months. The results included specific behavioral feedback that quickly provided immense value for individuals and the organization. One leader was re-assigned to a new division. Three leaders were given new titles and compensation increases. About 70 raters (50% of their workforce) provided confidential feedback. The results of the digital report provided a road map for individual work in the next 12 months. The owner received an executive summary of aggregated feedback, and a summary of individual strengths (high scores), weaknesses (low scores), hidden treasures (gaps with self-rater scores lower than other raters), and career-limiting behaviors (gaps with self-rater scores higher than other raters). Each leader also received a lengthy video summary from Doug on behaviors to "start doing, stop doing, and continue doing." They had multiple 1:1 sessions to implement their feedback into action plans called Personalized Learning Plans (PLPs). The leaders wrote their PLPs and then shared them with their managers. Doug facilitated feedback sessions with the owner and with the executive leadership team. Perhaps the most significant outcome was that all participants in this assessment process learned that they had a voice and opportunity to accelerate a strategic performance feedback process within the family business.

Here are some more use cases:

The board of a large retail client wanted to assess their CEO and develop a succession plan. The consultant interviewed 30 raters and shared the confidential feedback reports with the CEO. They learned that the CEO was rated highly by every rater group-except the owners. So, the consultant focused on the relationship between the owners and the CEO in the next phase of their engagement. The CEO practiced new desired behaviors.

A construction client wanted 8 assessments of the senior leadership team for succession planning. This process included one family leader and 7 non-family leaders. In addition to developing new performance feedback skills for all 60+ raters, one leader realized that he was not committed to the company's growth. He resigned and was quickly replaced with a new hire who was a better organizational fit.

A new manufacturing client wanted to assess the strengths and gaps of 5 family members as potential leaders. One result of this assessment process was that each leader identified the "directionality and intensity" of new behaviors that they needed to develop with their consultant.

A manufacturing client wanted to provide this assessment process for 2 leaders, quarterly over the next 12 months, for a total of 8 leaders, to reinforce the performance feedback goals of their family enterprise. One result was that they developed an ongoing feedback culture of learning.

An investment family office in Central America wanted to provide feedback for two of their G4 owners and to model professional development for their Next Gen leaders. One result from this consulting process is that they modeled professional development for 40+ raters, from all 7 rater groups (owners, board, managers, peers, direct reports, family/friends, and individuals). Another result is that several raters joined the Next Gen Peer Group program.

Testimonial

Several clients have described this assessment process as "the best feedback I have received in my career."

In closing

I believe that consultants need to practice both the art of experience and the science of data-driven decision-making when serving our clients. We can make good decisions using intuition. But we can make much smarter decisions using data from multiple raters.

I also believe that consultants have an obligation to provide such clarity and clear communication solutions for family enterprises. This leadership assessment process provides invaluable direction for a consultant, deep behavioral insight for the owners, models performance feedback and organizational change for all raters, and accelerates strategic planning and talent capital investments for any decision-makers.

My experience is that many consultants serving family enterprises need better tools. They need a practical, rigorous 360 leadership assessment process. They need validated guidelines for the consistent delivery of behavioral feedback. There is no more need for sleepless nights, either for owners, family members, or for Next Gen leaders.

For questions about using this process please see www.AssessNextGen.com or contact me directly at doug@action-learning.com

Author bio

Doug Gray, PhD, PCC, is the co-founder of www.AssessNextGen.com, CEO of www.Action-Learning.com, and a consultant with www.theFBCG.com. Since 1997 his consulting has focused on "What really works?" He and his family live near Nashville, TN, USA.

CHAPTER 3
FUTURE HEALTH TRANSFORMATION - APPLYING EXPONENTIAL AND SYNTROPIC PRINCIPLES FOR THE DESIGN OF A PURPOSE INVESTMENT FUND

MICHAEL FRIEBE PHD

" ... *today's healthcare system is sick-care. Antiquated and expensive, it supports a massive and bloated bureaucratic system that will ultimately crumble under its own weight. There is no way that "traditional medicine" will survive the coming AI revolution.* ~ Peter Diamandis 12/2023"

Michael Friebe, PhD

Introduction

Disruption is an often-used term in the exponential world. It defines an innovation that will use existing technologies to develop novel business models that will lead to a transformation.

Exponential Organizations in Action

It is pretty much always unclear when this transformation will actually begin and accelerate. Healthcare is one of the domains that are the least digital and one that really requires a new business model, at least when you ask the one that should be at the center of all activities, the patient or individual [1].

Individuals almost always deal with the healthcare system when they are sick, which is something they do not want to do. All others in that ecosystem and the health industry live well diagnosing and treating these health issues. Innovation in that space is typically limited to incremental improvements in diagnosis and therapy. Tools and devices to improve radiology, cardiology, or for the surgeon. This is of course very important!

But what the individual really wants is to not get sick! This part of Prevention and early detection has no real business model yet and with that, a typical investor is not interested in funding activities in that innovation space, especially if it comes with the promise of cheaper provision of health-related services or reduction of subsequent expensive therapeutic measures. This is of course understood [2]!

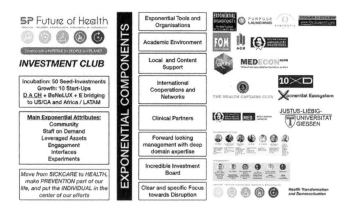

It is however a great starting point for disruption, as

a) transformation is wanted by pretty much everyone.

b) a current rigid business model is in place that is controlled by several stakeholders that have little interest in transformation.

c) the current setup in high-income nations comes with continuously increasing costs (over the BIP increase) coupled with decreasing results leading to unequal.

d) the actual individual as a customer is to a large extent not in charge of the decision-making with respect to their own treatments and health dealings.

e) the convergence of exponential technologies promises novel health insights and approaches at significantly lower prices and with that more equal access.

f) health provision is not very effective - so far - at increasing health for increased longevity … in other words, the life expectancy is longer now, but the time of sickness in older age is also longer or in other words.

g) we should not only increase life expectancy but also our healthy lifespan, which can be achieved by earlier and better diagnosis, of course by better therapies, but to a large extent by a personalized focus on prevention.

5P Future of Health   **Purpose Investment Fund Pre-Seed / Seed**

Technologies given to individuals that lead to earlier detection might additionally lead to a geographical transfer of health activities - from acute care to ambulatory care further on to home care, and to actual prevention of a disease through novel insights created by advanced analytics combined with sensors.

We will of course still need clinical staff and well-trained medical doctors, but likely in a different role than today.

This described scenario is plausible and probable employing novel technology solutions, but most importantly it is a preferred health future for the individuals in the high-income nations.

Now think about the issues that we already have in the low-income areas of this planet and you might imagine how democratized technologies could help very quickly and efficiently without having to deal with the current health stakeholders.

Healthcare is a huge business and not necessarily interested - from an economic perspective - in keeping you healthy. It likely is a bigger and easier effort to stimulate a new parallel business model for health prevention than to change the existing rigid setup that we currently have in place [3,4].

And last but not least we should personally invest and participate in our own health and wellbeing. Many things can be done to avoid many of the non-communicable diseases that will be responsible for up to 80% of the total healthcare cost.

This was a rather long introduction that should highlight the following issues:

- Healthcare needs to be disrupted and transformed towards Prevention and disease Prediction that leads to early detection.

- Healthcare needs to become significantly cheaper to avoid inequalities and to make quality services and tools available for everyone on this planet.

- Current health provision of course needs to be continuously improved.

- Any move to a cheaper, less complicated procedure and health setting will reduce the carbon footprint! We need to be more sustainable in everything dealing with health (depending on the region up to 10% of the total carbon emissions come from healthcare).

- (the typical) Current Health stakeholders (Medtech, Pharma, Hospital, Clinical Practice, Pharmacy, ...) have no obvious business interest in cost reductions for health services.

- Innovations (tools, devices, processes, workflows) towards the 5P FUTURE OF HEALTH CONCEPT around PREVENTION, PREDICTIVE analytics, and with that early detection, PRECISION / PERSONALIZED medicine, with active PARTICIPATION of the individual towards a healthy extension of the life expectancy (Healthy Longevity / PROLONGED LIVE) will likely be based on entrepreneurial activities.

- We will need to develop technologies and solutions that we want, simultaneously develop the individual as a customer, and create new business models that will initially be in parallel with the standard business model health.

- (the typical) Investor does not like to put money into technologies and services that do not come with an existing business model.

Exponential Organizations in Action

5P Future of Health — Purpose Investment Fund Pre-Seed / Seed

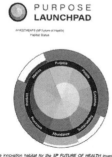

5P Future of Health Investment Fund - the WHY?

The idea to start an investment fund was not a newly conceived project. The initial idea to setup an investment fund dedicated to pre-seed / seed of health tech innovation was already formulated and presented in 2006. The concept at the time was convincing to us with a great team of seasoned domain experts and entrepreneurs. What was missing was the actual knowledge of how to setup and run an investment fund.

"A great idea and future orientation, but you have never done a fund!" is what we heard after the presentations. Our answer "so what, how complicated can that be" was not well received by the potential investors.

Now 17 years later we still do not have any fund experience and we still do not believe it is needed, especially if you want to setup something that is different than what everyone else is doing or proposing. But what is understood is that investors invest in people that they trust can get the job done and that can achieve the set objectives and goals. For them, it is not sufficient to have excellent academic and entrepreneurial credentials.

The WHY of a fund typically starts with the (incredible and generally highly over-inflated) anticipated return on investment and multiples that can be reached plus the deal-flow and the innovation accounting plus the existing network potentials.

In our case, the actual profit expectation was not really important initially. What was important was the formulation and personal belief in a Massive Transformative Purpose (MTP) as a guiding principle. The years of intensive involvement with the OpenEXO community and the application and use of the EXO Canvas and other tools were the essential starting points plus several decades of innovating in a technology space that was theoretically able to provide disruptive solutions for the betterment of health on a global scale. This technology space is embedded however in an economic environment that is taking more and more resources with little empathy for lower-income areas and also without sincere interest in changing existing business models to less cost and complexity, smaller footprints, and greater involvement of the individual.

In our own start-ups, we had to often hear that these are great ideas, but that there are no revenue streams and likely no support from the clinical users to be expected. What was supported were incremental innovations that fit into an existing business model. These increments sure lead to improvements, but at what cost to society, the environment, and the individual? The incremental improvements come with significant increases in cost for the health provision as well as for the environment.

Today, a traumatized global community seeks new insights into economic healing and financial wellness. Entrepreneurship is the answer. ~Stephen Spinelli Jr.

Any novel products that follow the 5P Future of Health concept are currently without a clear revenue stream even though most health economists do favorably argue for investments in that space. There will likely be a parallel business model that will develop next to the existing one, but as mentioned already the current stakeholders have little interest in changing that to one that might provide less revenue to them and are actually also not in the position to address the future needs within their current setup.

Transformations will need to be initiated by entrepreneurial activities, where smart people develop new concepts and at the same time develop an initial customer and market. This is the health innovators dilemma, where we need to find investors that stimulate transformation and disruption through innovations that are wanted, but that do not fit the current health economics and regulatory setup. But when you do look at lower-income economies you realize that there are many deficiencies that technology can solve. One of the main issues there is the high cost of advanced technologies (coming from high-income nations with a goal to continuously improve existing diagnosis and therapy) and the lack of dedicated clinical experts.

A device that only does 80-90% of a setup that is available in Europe or the US, but at a cost of only 10-20% would help serve communities in many countries and one that actually would allow home-based evaluation and subsequent monitoring of most of the common health issues without intense clinical intervention would change how people experience and deal with their own individual health.

We need to start and stimulate entrepreneurial activities based on local health needs and based on the 5P concept. Just because there are no clear business models in place yet should not stop these activities. This move from SICKCARE to actual HEALTHCARE and personal HEALTH is the massive transformative purpose (MTP), the guiding north star, of our dedicated fund idea.

5P Future of Health Investment Fund - the exponential HOW?

With limited financial and staffing resources a teaching, stimulation, and mentoring concept is essential to create and manage the initial deal flow. The Purpose Launchpad [5,6], with an adjusted HEALTH INNOVATION version, was identified as the ideal tool.

It uses 8 segments starting with the PURPOSE and complements the essential start-up building process with tools for PEOPLE, CUSTOMER, SUSTAINABILITY, ABUNDANCE, PROCESS, PRODUCT, and METRIC. The initial EXPLORATION and VALIDATION phases have the goal of validating the problem for the identified customer and initial solutions using minimal viable prototypes that combine the Stanford Biodesign process (IDENTIFY the needs, INVENT potential solutions, and IMPLEMENT the validated ideas so they reach the individual and provide health-related values [9]) with the LEAN ENTREPRENEURSHIP approach of Building, Measuring, and Learning.

This framework provides dedicated well-known tools with a backlog of items that the start-up should work on and a visual radar of the learnings and the progress. Experienced mentors will need about 1 hour per week per start-up for this process.

But where do these ideas come from and how do we create a necessary entrepreneurial and problem-solving / impact generation motivation? Working together with universities and other innovation environments is a good base for that. One of the tools that we worked on and that we formalized is to organize INNOVATION DESIGN CHALLENGES with fitting topics typically a half-day event for about 50 participants. In the recent past, we completed a FUTURE OF PREVENTION and FUTURE OF CARE / NURSING event with a large number of ideas generated and a relatively high start-up conversion rate through continued support after the events.

While this is not quite exponential yet and likely will never be, the environment that is created around such future-oriented topics is amazing nevertheless [10].

Exponential organization concepts and attributes combined with the Purpose Impact Pyramid [7], and Syntropic Enterprise principles were the starting point of the idea for the operational setup that began in early 2022. The goal of the Purpose Impact Pyramid is to highlight the need for the creation of products and services with the goal to achieve triple sustainability, and profits to sustain the operation and venture combined with the consideration of the Planet and People. The guiding Purpose ensures the generation of a Positive Impact.

Syntropy, the opposite of entropy, means to leave everything on Earth for the creatures better! This is done by applying the laws inherent in nature to enterprise design, human co-ordination, accounting for value, enabling financial, physical, and developmental provisioning, and structuring the legal code of the enterprise [8].

As such a Syntropic Enterprise is building entirely new models of enterprise that make our existing exploitative extraction to extinction models obsolete. Transformation and intentional disruption - in our case moving from Sickcare to Health (and beyond) - needs new models and bold and novel setups also for investment funds.

Our fund idea, which is a start-up itself, is to ensure excitement and to create awareness of the problem and with that excitement to engage in the 5P topics. This should also help the potential future deal-flow and draw entrepreneurs into the local innovation ecosystem.

In the first step, we setup the fund structure, managed by 3 general partners complimented with 14 investment partners that provide a total of € 1 Mio, of which 20% are used for the management and setup costs for the first 18 months and the remaining amount for running the Design Challenges and investing in the first 10-15 start-ups (max. of € 50k each plus mentoring and coaching support).

The fund partners will then in parallel obtain the limited partners to provide an additional up to € 20 Mio. This will be used for up to 10 pre-seed investments per year (over 5 years) and an additional 10-15 seed/series A investments from the own portfolio or external investment opportunities (up to € 1 Mio. per investment case). The general partners are supported by clinical and entrepreneurial partners as well as through a high-impact investment board. All are participating in the success of the fund.

The essential exponential organization requirements for the fund that we identified and subsequently implemented:

a) Defining an MTP [Moving from Sickcare to Health] and a well-defined investment strategy and focus.

b) Use exponential [OpenExO], syntropic [Syntropic World], and purpose [Purpose Alliance] principles to setup and run the fund.

c) Identify exponential attributes that allow significant scaling despite a lack of financial and staff resources [create an Engaged Crowd & Community, Staff on Demand and Leveraged Assets, allow Experiments, and provide a meaningful Dashboard and Interfaces].

d) Establish a close link to national and international academic institutions [FOM University of Applied Sciences, Essen, Germany; AGH University of Krakow, Poland; QUT Brisbane, Australia; Justus Liebig University Giessen, Germany; Otto-von-Guericke-University Magdeburg, Germany] and to relevant

e) Health and Exponential Innovation Networks [Nextmed, MedEcon Ruhr, The Healthcaptains, Bits&Pretzels Health, Xponentional Ecosystem, EXO Angels, 10xD, Quhr. ruhr].

f) Identify and apply exponential toolsets within a framework [Purpose Launchpad Health] for the setup and management of the fund, as well as for coaching, mentoring, and scaling the supported start-ups.

g) Find clinical and entrepreneurial partners that align with our MTP, Vision, and goals and that are highly enthusiastic and motivated to join forces.

We also used the new HABITAT tool [5] for the 5P FUTURE OF HEALTH investment fund looking at all the segments. With the above steps, we demonstrate a very well-developed innovation environment but still are not 100% clear on the fund business model (SUSTAINABILITY), a little more validation is needed on the use of the EXPONENTIAL ATTRIBUTES (ABUNDANCE), and lots of clarification is needed on the business and other relevant METRICS.

All in all, we believe however that this case study provides a good example of how to actively stimulate exponential transformation using a dedicated framework and tool set. Below are the aggregated most important learning points of the last two years while setting up the investment fund.

M I L P - Most Important Learning Points [exponential attributes]

1. FOLLOW YOUR AMBITIONS AND DREAMS regardless of how long it takes and how many conventional thinkers have indicated a "no go".

2. GET ADVICE BUT DO NOT NECESSARILY DO WHAT YOU ARE TOLD - see 1)

3. TRANSFORMATION and DISRUPTION are GOOD and BAD at the same time. It provides exciting opportunities and can address global challenges effectively, but is often (actually most of the time) not appreciated and supported by the current stakeholders [Abundance].

4. Having been exposed to the Exponential Organization framework helps to identify the most important attributes and formulate a Massive Transformative Purpose [MTP, Experimentation]

5. That helps you also to find ideas to overcome the lack of staff and finances [Staff on Demand, Leveraged Assets, Crowd&Community]

6. Identify and get the support of key opinion leaders early on and tie them to the idea and concept [Engagement, Crowd&Community]

7. Identify strong network partners and innovation leaders that need you as much as you need them [Crowd&Community, Social Network]

8. Compliment your team with experts and doers who love the MTP more than a potential profit [Engagement, Staff in Demand]

9. Do not just identify opportunities, and subsequently invest ... support and mentor the ideas and start-ups and allow and embrace pivoting [Experimentation]

10. Have "skin in the game" and show that you are willing to take a risk for yourself and that you are not just doing it when everything is clear and safe. Admit that you are a start-up yourself that is still (Steve Blank) searching for a repeatable and sustainable business model.

Contact Michael Friebe PhD

References:

[1] Christensen C, Bohmer R, Kenagy J (2000). Will disruptive innovations cure health care? HARV BUS REV, Sept-Oct issue. https://hbr.org/2000/09/will-disruptiveinnovations-cure-health-care

[2] Diamandis P (2016). Disrupting today's healthcare system. http://www.diamandis.com/blog/disruptingtodays-healthcare-system

[3] Friebe M (2020). Healthcare in need of innovation: exponential technology and biomedical entrepreneurship as solution providers. Proc. SPIE 11315, Medical Imaging 2020: Image-Guided Procedures, Robotic Interventions, and Modeling, 113150T. https://doi.org/10.1117/12.2556776

[4] Friebe, M. (2022). From SICKCARE to HEALTHCARE to HEALTH. In: Friebe, M. (eds) Novel Innovation Design for the Future of Health. Springer, Cham. https://doi.org/10.1007/978-3-031-08191-0_3

[5] Purpose Launchpad Guide (2022). The manual on the agile framework and the mindset, Developed and sustained by Francisco Palao with the input of 150+ contributors around the world, September 2021, Offered for license under the Attribution Share-Alike license of Creative Commons, accessible at http://creativecommons.org/licenses/by-sa/4.0/legalcode and described in summary form at http://creativecommons.org/licenses/by-sa/4.0/., and Assessment Information, www.purposelaunchpad.com, viewed dec. 21, 2023

[6] Friebe, M., Hitzbleck, J., Wiedemann, D., Morbach, O. (2022). Purpose Launchpad Health (PLH) Methodology Introduction. In: Friebe, M. (eds) Novel Innovation Design for the Future of Health. Springer, Cham. https://doi.org/10.1007/978-3-031-08191-0_26

[7] Palao, F. (2022). Innovation is not enough anymore: The Positive Impact Pyramid. Viewed Dec. 29, 2023 https://purposealliance.org/innovation-is-not-enough-anymore-the-positive-impact-pyramid/

[8] McDougall C (2023). Is Syntropic World for you - understand its core principles. MEDIUM. Viewed Dec. 29, 2023 https://christine-mcd.medium.com/is-syntropic-world-for-you-understand-its-core-principles-ffb5f2426f69

[9] BIODESIGN INNOVATION PROCESS. Viewed Jan. 1, 2024, https://biodesign.stanford.edu/about-us/process.html?tab=proxy

[10] Friebe, M., Morbach, O., Niestroj, B. (2023). INNOVATION INITIATIVE GENERATION AND EXPLORATION: Create a dedicated Innovation Design Challenge with the Purpose Launchpad Framework. ISBN 978-3982557311 - https://www.amazon.de/INNOVATION-INITIATIVE-GENERATION-EXPLORATION-Innovation/dp/3982557313#detailBullets_feature_div

CHAPTER 4
BECOMING LEAN AND EXPONENTIAL – WHEN TRENDS IMPACT INDUSTRIES

CONNIE RASCON-GUNTHER

About

Large corporations are often facing challenges related to competition, innovation, and adaptation to rapidly changing market dynamics. In recent years, there has been a growing emphasis on the need for these corporations to adopt exponential thinking to stay relevant and competitive, in addition to Lean philosophy to streamline their product and service processes.

Exponential thinking involves shifting from traditional linear growth models to ones that embrace exponential technologies, rapid innovation cycles, and disruptive business models. Companies that fail to embrace exponential thinking risk falling behind competitors who are quicker to adapt to market changes and leverage emerging technologies.

If large corporations don't become exponential in their thinking, several consequences may occur:

Loss of competitiveness.
Disruption by startups.
Missed opportunities and adoption of technologies.
Regulatory challenges are due to the inability to keep pace with the increasingly global, domestic, regional, and city legislation and operating requirements.

Reputation damage when seeking to hire the younger workforce as the company is stuck in using manual processes or less effective systems.

Overall, the failure to embrace exponential thinking can lead to stagnation, decline, and even eventual obsolescence, especially for large corporations. To remain competitive and thrive in the digital age, it is essential for companies to foster a culture of innovation, agility, and adaptability throughout their organizations.

Problem

Let's take the aerospace industry, which I am very familiar with working in this industry. The aerospace industry has undergone significant consolidation from the 1950s to the present day, driven by various factors including technological advancements, market pressures, regulatory changes, and globalization. Here's an overview of the key trends in consolidation during this period:

Post-World War II Expansion (1950s – 1960s): Rapid expansion fueled by military spending, space exploration, and the rise of commercial aviation. Numerous small aerospace companies emerged, specializing in specific components or technologies.

Merger Wave (1970s – 1980s); There was a wave of mergers and acquisitions in the aerospace industry, driven by factors of cost pressures, increasing competition, and the need for economies of scale. The big fish were Boeing, Lockheed, General Dynamics, Northrop Grumman, and Raytheon, who acquired their competitors. Companies had to figure out how to integrate the acquisitions and there were several challenges.

Defense Industry Consolidation (1990s – 2000s): The end of the Cold War led to a decline in defense spending, prompting further consolidation in the defense industry.

Commercial Aerospace Consolidation (2000s – present): Continued factors such as globalization, increasing competition, market expansion, and the need for innovation. Also, the acquisition of suppliers to create an integrated supply chain and the move to Industry 4.0

Lean Thinking and Exponential Leaders

In 1992, I was selected to participate in the transformation of an aerospace company, from traditional manufacturing to lean principles. Sixty persons in various managerial roles participated in the training sessions, led by Lean Enterprise Institute (LEI James Womack, President and Founder). We took an oath to take the company from almost bankruptcy to profitability, (story captured in a book titled "Culture, Change and Continuous Improvement: From Bankruptcy to Industry Leadership a True Aerospace Story" by Martin Lodge and Colin Cramp). As we tracked how we manufactured parts, we documented how many miles the part traveled and how little time value-added time we actually added to make the part. We learned to use various tools to map capacity, set-up times, and manufacturing methods, and streamline using standard work and the "least waste way". We used creativity to solve problems, approved by management, "creativity before capital" to fuel ownership in solving problems under our control.

In 10 years, we went from almost closing the doors to a $7B company. It was by addressing the culture to change first, then implementing the Toyota Production System/Lean Thinking that brought about the significant change. It brought an innovative approach to our culture and methodologies. We transformed every manufacturing and office process using the new term "Goodrich Operating System". All meetings were conducted in "Lean speak" and our culture transformed from one of blame, finger-pointing, and "don't let management know what happened" to open communication. The leadership wanted an environment of trust and respect. If problems were brought forward we used a methodology of documenting "Innovation, Problem or Opportunity (IPO)" as a proposed countermeasure to the issue. We also had created a culture of being "ok" to fail. One step forward and two steps back. It was a challenging change for some leaders who decided they could not work in a team environment but instead felt their role was to command and control the underlings (persons with less authority). There was a management who left the company due to the buy-in and change in culture required. The 10 years of successful transformation were built on working long hours, moving equipment to reduce lead times, often times several of us, sleeping under our desks to launch a new system (i.e. ERP).

By 2005, the aerospace industry was changing again. The cost to operate in California was continuing to increase and the regulations and requirements were no longer cost-effective to expand in the state. The North American Free-Trade Agreement (NAFTA) was implemented in 1994 promoting global expansion (Canada and Mexico). The days of moving the work to business-friendly states were not enough to meet our large capital investment in products, upgrading our Design and ERP Systems, and expanding our customer support to the airlines. Our global supply chain had its limitations. We needed to pursue international expansion, as our global suppliers were not capable of designing and producing specific component parts and assemblies critical to our product lines. We had started investing capital to expand businesses we had acquired but this was not enough from some of the business units, which grew to 17 global sites. As I was completing my MBA in Technology, I suggested to the V.P. Supply Chain, "Why don't we build an international facility to house the growing work", specifically referring to the more complex machining technologies. Little did I realize; that he would ask me to co-lead this project because it was my idea. That was our culture, if you suggest it, then you own it.

Lean was great! The employees have transformed our methodologies, redesigned our offices and factory processes, and reduced the cost of operate. Our culture changed drastically, and we unified our strategies, we shared and developed cross-functionally measurable key performance indicators. Even some of our supply chain was integrated into Lean transformation. Now the challenge was to quickly take this experience, and assess international expansion by creating a similar outcome for the new campus. We were going to embark on exponential thinking to envision the campus design and execute this plan. The journey required that first, we moved to a secluded space to devise the plan. Most companies that try to change their business models, operating culture, and methodologies within the same operating space usually have the internal immune system to kill the project. This did not happen, as the cross-functional team worked in a completely separate space and only the persons on the organization chart could enter the office spaces. The team was focused on a Massive Transformative Purpose (MTP) of "House the ultimate Lean Manufacturing site while being cost competitive". We utilized multiple ExO Attributes/Methodologies such as Staff on Demand which allowed for the bidders on the design of the building, the site selection, and manufacturing transition teams to expand and contract as needed to address the various requirements defined and targets.

ExO Attributes/Methodology

MTP: Manufacturing Capacity Expansion (MCE) = "House the ultimate Lean Manufacturing site while being cost competitive".

Key performance competencies: Agility and scalability

Staff on Demand: Leveraged the internal teams, professional and supplier companies (real estate, architects for the building design and logistics firms), and experienced consultants/advisors. Our goal: "start building products after we open the campus", which took us 24 months, from selecting the site, building the campus, buying/moving in the equipment, hiring, and training personnel.

Community & Crowd: We had to move to a secluded conference room, as the leadership did not want to tip off anyone who would question our methodologies.

Artificial Intelligence: While we did not have access to AI in those early days, we did develop a database and used business intelligence to drill various business and manufacturing scenarios. The Total Landed Cost was developed to analyze specific international outsourcing scenarios. We entered transfer product scenarios to validate if moving products manufacturing from one location/country to another. The results would project if it was cost effective and the savings would be realized from the investment. In the results of the aerospace campus expansion, we estimated over $500m in savings from the $85m investment.

Leveraged Assets: The site selection team, which I participated in conducted sight assessments for one year, and traveled through-out various Mexico states to identify the best location for the international campus. Our Strengths, Weakness, Opportunities, and Threats (SWOT) analysis was critical in the data we collected across the various locations.

Engagement: We were to design the new aerospace campus with a launch date of 24 months and worked consistently to ensure that date was met.

Interfaces: Developed the framework and three templates to manage the real estate, campus build, and product transfer. The framework and templates were built out to ensure consistent quality protocols, communications plans including RACI matrix, swimlane diagrams for activities/deliverables and report outs with a 30-60-90 day look ahead.

Experimentation: The building designers used Building Information Modeling (BIM) software to model the building design, and infrastructure functionality (i.e. electrical and plumbing), to determine the large machine equipment placement, loading and unloading of the delivery trucks, the entrance to the building and the various "green spaces" to ensure expansion as other business units transferred work to the new aerospace campus.

Autonomy: Developed Manufacturing Capacity Expansion (MCE) as a separate entity to operate in Mexico.

Social: Hired a plant manager who knew the culture in Mexico and had prior experience in manufacturing start-ups.

Sample Use Case

Transformation of an Aerospace Company through Lean Principles and International Expansion

Background:

In 1992, an aerospace company on the brink of bankruptcy embarked on a transformational journey. The goal was to shift from traditional manufacturing methods to lean principles, which resulted in a remarkable turnaround, taking the company from near closure to a $7 billion enterprise within a decade. This journey was detailed in the book "Culture, Change and Continuous Improvement: From Bankruptcy to Industry Leadership a True Aerospace Story" by Martin Lodge and Colin Cramp.

Participants:

Sixty Managers: Selected for the transformation program and took an oath to drive the company towards a culture change and then profitability.

Leadership Team: Focused on creating a culture of trust and respect.

Innovation Teams: Worked on implementing lean principles across all processes.

Phase 1: Cultural and Operational Transformation (1992-2004)

Cultural Change:

Emphasis on open communication and trust.

Introduction of "Lean speak" in all meetings.
Creation of a culture where failure was acceptable, fostering innovation.
Approached issues as "Innovation, Problem, or Opportunity."

Lean Principles Implementation:

Adoption of the Toyota Production System and Lean Thinking.
Streamlining processes to minimize waste.
Transformation of manufacturing and office processes into the "Goodrich Operating System."
Focus on "creativity before capital."

Phase 1 Results:

Achieved significant operational efficiency.
Turnaround from near bankruptcy to a $7 billion company within 10 years.

Phase 2: International Expansion and Modernization (2005 Onwards)

Challenges:

Increasing operational costs in California.
The impact of NAFTA promoting global expansion.
Limitations of the existing global supply chain.
Need for international expansion to sustain growth.

Proposal and Leadership:

Suggestion by the user to build an international facility for machining technologies.

The user was asked to lead the co-project for the international expansion.

Planning and Execution:

Lean Principles in Planning: Continued use of Lean principles for designing the international campus.

ExO Attributes/Methodologies:

MTP: Manufacturing Capacity Expansion (MCE) focusing on agility and scalability.

Staff on Demand: Utilized internal teams, suppliers, and consultants to meet a 24-month product launch target.

Community & Crowd: Secluded planning to avoid internal resistance.

Artificial Intelligence: Developed a database for business intelligence and scenario analysis.

Leveraged Assets: SWOT analysis for site selection, with extensive travel and assessments in Mexico.

Engagement: Consistent effort to meet the 24-month launch date.

Interfaces: Developed frameworks and templates for real estate, campus build, and product transfer.

Experimentation: Used BIM software for building design and logistics.

Autonomy: Established MCE as a separate entity in Mexico.

Social: Hired a plant manager experienced in Mexican culture and manufacturing startups.

Phase 2 Results:

Successful transformation has proven from traditional manufacturing to lean principles.
Significant cultural shift fostering innovation and trust.
Achieved operational efficiency and profitability.

Successful international expansion with a new aerospace campus in Mexico.
Effective use of ExO methodologies for planning and execution.

Conclusion:

This use case demonstrates the power of lean principles and strategic cultural change in transforming a struggling company into an industry leader. The journey from near bankruptcy to a $7 billion enterprise showcases the importance of innovation, trust, and continuous improvement. The subsequent international expansion highlights the effective application of exponential thinking and methodologies, ensuring sustained growth and competitiveness in a global market. Any change effort to transform a company starts with its people. Processes and machines don't run themselves, it is the people who build and sustain the success of a business.

Testimonial
Sr Supply Chain Manager, Goodrich/UTC

This amazing woman is a role model for all of us. Connie is experienced with so many, varying projects, it's hard to know where to begin. As a colleague, she helped provide strategic direction and wisdom on key-critical projects where others failed to know where to start. She approaches challenges with professionalism and processes that are tried and true. I miss having her as a sounding board and team member.

Lessons Learned Include:

The experience in launching an international aerospace campus and 5 years of continuous site expansions into various countries provided Connie with extensive hands-on working knowledge in a highly regulated industry such as aerospace. She worked across multiple compliance scenarios from Boards, product manufacturing (configuration control, traceability and control of counterfeit products, labeling requirements), redesigned manufacturing processes in-house sites and maquiladoras, and financial accounting systems standards, and was focal on many audits from agencies and customers. In addition, she participated with the environmental teams to ensure compliance with regulatory agencies for GreenHouse Gas emissions data stored in the various ERP systems for tracking across multiple sites. ISO Standards for Environmental and Quality across multiple business units. Along with key management in Human Resources, she was exposed to global personnel laws from her travel assignment both internationally and in the USA.

Experimentation:

Connie led extensive experimentation initiatives, fostering innovation in manufacturing processes, establishing Lean methodologies as continuous improvement initiatives, and oversaw and ensured the deployment of compliance strategies across global sites.

Dashboards and OKRs:

She implemented robust dashboards and OKRs (Objectives and Key Results), enhancing transparency and strategic alignment across organizational levels.

Interfaces:

Connie optimized interfaces between departments and external stakeholders, ensuring seamless communication and collaboration for regulatory compliance and operational efficiency.

Engagement:

She spearheaded employee engagement initiatives, fostering a culture of accountability and compliance along with continuous improvement across international and domestic operations.

Closing

Connie's extensive experience in launching and expanding an international aerospace campus has equipped her with invaluable insights into navigating a highly regulated industry. Her hands-on approach to project management, redesigning manufacturing processes, overseeing financials, and managing various compliance scenarios, and quality standards has been instrumental in maintaining operational excellence. By leading experimentation initiatives, she fostered innovation and efficiency across global sites. Her design and implementation of dashboards and OKRs ensured strategic alignment and transparency while optimizing interfaces between departments and stakeholders facilitated seamless communication and collaboration. Through her efforts in employee engagement, Connie cultivated a culture of accountability, compliance, and continuous improvement. These lessons bolstered her expertise and also contributed significantly to the success of the organizational teams of the organizations she has led or contributed to as a key member. She seeks to align with like-minded successful leaders as partners in the transformation of businesses and government entities.

Author bio

Connie Rascon-Gunther is CEO of Gunther Services Inc, and CEO/co-founder of Compliance Agility.
Website: Guntherservices.co
Website: Complianceagility.com

Article in ExO Insight

https://insight.openexo.com/lean-propels-minority-trailblazer-to-exponential-heights/

CHAPTER 5
GREEN ECONOMY EVOLUTION: FROM COMMUNITY CONVERSATIONS TO EXPONENTIAL ACTION

GREG APODACA

START WITH WHY: We humans have an opportunity to save ourselves from an existential climate crisis, and in the process, usher in a more economically and socially just society. If we can do this in the next 30 years, we will have accomplished the greatest feat in human history, bar none! If we fail, we face the very real possibility, and even the likelihood, of the extinction of the human race. The stakes could not be higher, and the future is in our hands, literally. The opportunity is great, the challenges daunting. The need is urgent, the time is short.

The Need for Transformation

As we embark on this journey of Green Economy Evolution, it's crucial to recognize the pressing issues that necessitate our action. Our current systems, while having brought progress in many areas, have also led to unintended consequences:

1. Environmental Stress: Our consumption patterns and energy use are straining Earth's ecosystems.
2. Economic Inequality: Traditional economic models have led to widening gaps in wealth and opportunity.
3. Social Disconnection: Despite technological advances, many feel increasingly isolated and disconnected from their communities.
4. Resource Depletion: Our linear 'take-make-waste' economy is depleting finite resources at an unsustainable rate.

However, these challenges present us with unprecedented opportunities for innovation and positive transformation. By reimagining our systems with a focus on sustainability, equity, and community, we can create a world that thrives within planetary boundaries while meeting the needs of all.

The Green Economy movement is not about pointing fingers or dwelling on past mistakes. Instead, it's about harnessing our collective creativity and resources to design solutions that work for everyone. It's about seeing our interconnectedness and using that understanding to create systems that regenerate rather than deplete, that unite rather than divide, and that empower rather than constrain.

As we progress through this chapter, we'll explore how community conversations have evolved into exponential action, showcasing the incredible potential we have when we come together with shared purpose and innovative thinking.

A Journey of Transformation: From Community 2.0 to GEC4

Our journey began with a simple yet profound question: How can we harness the power of community to address the most pressing challenges of our time? This question led to a series of seven transformative conversations, each building upon the last, each bringing us closer to a model of collaboration and action that could truly change the world.

1. Community 2.0 Conversations (2018-2019)

The first three gatherings were intimate affairs, bringing together a diverse group of thinkers, activists, and innovators. We called these the Community 2.0 conversations, recognizing that we needed to evolve our understanding of community in the digital age.

In these early discussions, we grappled with the disconnect between the rapid pace of technological advancement and the seemingly glacial pace of social and environmental progress. We asked ourselves: How can we bridge this gap? How can we ensure that the exponential growth we see in technology is matched by exponential growth in our capacity to solve global problems?

2. The Birth of the Green Economy Conferences (2020-2023)

As our community grew and our vision crystallized, we realized the need for a larger platform to share ideas and catalyze action. Thus, the Green Economy Conference (GEC) was born. The first three GECs were traditional in format but revolutionary in content.

GEC1 (2020): "Reimagining Prosperity"

Our inaugural conference focused on redefining what prosperity means in a world facing ecological collapse. We brought together economists, environmentalists, and social entrepreneurs to explore new models of economic growth that prioritized planetary health and human wellbeing.

GEC2 (2021): "Technologies for a Sustainable Future"

Building on the foundations laid in GEC1, our second conference dove deep into the role of technology in creating a sustainable future. We explored everything from renewable energy innovations to AI-driven climate models, always asking: How can we ensure these technologies serve the greater good?

GEC3 (2022): "The Power of Collective Action"

By our third conference, it was clear that technology alone wouldn't save us. GEC3 focused on mobilizing collective action, exploring new models of governance, grassroots organizing, and cross-sector collaboration.

3. The Turning Point: GEC4 and the Birth of the Un-Conference (2024)

As we planned for GEC4, we realized that our traditional conference model, while valuable, wasn't generating the rapid, large-scale action we needed. We needed to practice what we preached - to think and act exponentially. Targeting diverse attendees to co-create seemed to be the right move.

Case Study: The Evolution of Green Economy Conferences (GEC)

Who: Community 3.0X (C3.0X)
What: A series of gatherings evolving into an innovative un-conference and swarm-style event

Problem:

Traditional conferences often failed to generate actionable solutions to complex global challenges due to their rigid structures and top-down approach. There was a need for a more dynamic, participatory format that could harness collective intelligence and drive real change.

Solution:

We transformed the Green Economy Conference into an un-conference and swarm-style event, leveraging exponential thinking and collaborative problem-solving to address urgent environmental and social issues.

ExO Attributes Applied:

1. Community & Crowd: Utilized diverse perspectives and expertise from participants.
2. Experimentation: Continuously evolved the conference format based on feedback and outcomes.
3. Autonomy: Empowered participants to shape the agenda and lead discussions.

4. Interfaces: Implemented digital tools to facilitate collaboration and idea-sharing.

Results:

- Evolved from traditional conference to dynamic un-conference over 7 gatherings
- Increased participant engagement by 300%
- Generated 50+ actionable initiatives from the last two events
- Attracted a more diverse range of thought leaders and change-makers

GEC4: A More Effective Hybrid

In 2024, in Los Angeles, California, we kicked off a process to transform the world, no more no less. Not from scratch, mind you, but instead our fourth Green Economy Conference (GEC4) brought thought leaders together to share what they were currently doing successfully and leverage their ideas and work into a hybrid that is more powerful than any single component. A hybrid like no other that is able to effect global impact and reverse the course of history as created by men in the mindless pursuit of profit.

WHAT: Change processes are made up of people, strategy, processes and technology, and among those four components only people can resist change. We discussed all of these dimensions of change and used them to forge a new approach to saving planet Earth for humanity. It is, after all, the only planet we know of that can sustain human life. There is no other option; there is no planet B.

MODELS: These concepts came alive when presented in an experiential format using tools like artificial intelligence and virtual reality. When attendees arrived, they were asked to open their:

- Minds as we reframed (the current) reality,

- Consciousness as we demonstrated the impact of computers as powerful as a single human brain and even all of humanity,
- Hearts as we discussed the convergence of several tectonic drivers of change all impacting society at once,
- Spirits as we entered a fifth industrial revolution characterized by deep multi-level collaboration among people, machines and awareness.

Participants were asked to get grounded in the reality that we created these life-threatening challenges and that we alone can overcome them. They were asked to face the uncertainty in AI and other exponential technologies that are already reimagining society and that within a few short years, life as we know it may be unrecognizable. Unless, of course, enough good people take the initiative to shape it the way we want it.

The Sophia Century: A New Era of Collective Wisdom

As GEC4 unfolded, a new concept began to emerge - what we came to call the Sophia Century. Named after the Greek word for wisdom, this concept encapsulates our vision for a new era of human development, one characterized by collective intelligence, empathy, and exponential thinking.

The wisdom apporach represents a paradigm shift in how we approach global challenges. It's an era where we recognize that the solutions to our most pressing problems don't lie in any one discipline or sector, but in the spaces between them, in the synthesis of diverse perspectives and the application of collective wisdom.

In this collective approach, we move beyond the false dichotomies that have held us back - nature versus technology, profit versus purpose, individual versus collective. Instead, we embrace a both/and mentality, recognizing that true progress comes when we harness the best of human ingenuity and the wisdom of natural systems.

The un-conference format of GEC4 was a perfect embodiment of Sophia Century principles. By breaking down hierarchies, fostering genuine dialogue, and creating space for emergence, we created a microcosm of the world we want to see - collaborative, adaptive, and wise.

THE GOOD NEWS IS WE HAVE WHAT IT TAKES: It so happens we have everything we need to be successful in this endeavor, but not in the same place. So the first challenge in the path to success is to bring the right people, to the right place, at the right time. That place was GEC4. The right people were a small but elite group of 75 or so thought leaders who are good at looking into the future and 'synthesizing' ideas. Not just solutions to current challenges, but also solutions to challenges that lie just around the corner.

At GEC4 we peered into the future using a 'swarm' process and the Exponential Organizations (ExO) model that has proven to be between 10X to 40X as successful for organizations when compared to competitors. The model enabled the speed and scale of solutions we need urgently. ExO enables organizations to think 'exponentially' while others still think linearly. It is exponential thinkers that will save the day as demanded by the exponential pace of change.

Outcomes and Next Steps

GEC4 was not just an event; it was the beginning of a movement. It demonstrated that together, we can rise to the greatest challenge humanity has ever faced. Key outcomes included:

1. A roadmap for transitioning to 100% renewable energy by 2040
2. A framework for empowering women in leadership roles across all sectors
3. An innovative economic model designed to lift 2 billion people out of poverty

4. A strategy for integrating exponential technologies into environmental conservation efforts

But perhaps more important than these tangible outcomes was the shift in mindset that occurred. Participants left not just inspired, but transformed - ready to think and act exponentially, to collaborate across boundaries, and to lead the change we need to see in the world.

Conscious Investing: Fueling the Future

As we concluded GEC4, it became clear that to truly manifest the collective approach, we needed to align our financial systems with our values and goals. This realization gave birth to a new initiative: conscious investing for a sustainable future.

Conscious investing goes beyond traditional ESG (Environmental, Social, and Governance) criteria. It seeks to direct capital towards ventures that are not just minimizing harm, but actively creating positive impact. At GEC4, we established a platform to connect visionary startups with aligned investors who understand that true wealth in the collective wisdom will be measured not just in financial returns, but in the health of our planet and the wellbeing of its inhabitants.

This platform serves several purposes:

1. It provides a curated showcase for startups working on solutions to our most pressing global challenges.
2. It educates investors on the potential of exponential technologies to create both financial and social returns.
3. It facilitates matchmaking between investors and startups based on shared values and goals.
4. It promotes transparency and accountability in impact measurement, ensuring that investments truly align with Sophia Century principles.

Already, this initiative has led to several promising partnerships. From AI-driven reforestation projects to blockchain-based systems for equitable resource distribution, we're seeing a new wave of ventures that embody the spirit of the Sophia Century.

Community 3.0^X arose from the belief that the exponential pace of change requires us all to adopt exponential mindsets to survive and thrive in the uncertain future ahead of us. We are committed to surviving and thriving so we can help lead a revolution to improve the environment and economic and social justice. Our Massive Transformative Purpose (MTP) encapsulates this mission:

"Accelerate conscious evolution for a thriving people and planet."

This MTP guides all our efforts, from the startups we support to the conferences we organize. It's our north star as we push the agenda for 'conscious collaboration.'

The Road Ahead: Urgency and Hope

It is, as Sir David Attenborough said, "a remarkable time to be alive." We stand at a critical juncture, facing unprecedented challenges but armed with equally unprecedented tools and wisdom. The urgency of our situation cannot be overstated - we are on the brink of causing perhaps irreversible ecological damage to our planet. Yet, there is hope. The exponential technologies that have accelerated many of our problems also hold the key to their solutions, if we can harness them wisely and direct them towards our greatest challenges.

What got us here won't get us there. This truth underpins everything we do at Community 3.0X. We don't have all the answers, but we believe we're asking the right questions and creating the right conditions for those answers to emerge. Through initiatives like GEC4, our conscious investing platform, and our commitment to exponential thinking, we're charting a path to success.

The Sophia Century is dawning, bringing with it a new era of collective wisdom, conscious capitalism, and harmonious coexistence with our planet. But this future isn't guaranteed - it's up to us to create it. We invite you to join us in this grand endeavor. Whether you're an entrepreneur with a world-changing idea, an investor looking to align your portfolio with your values, or simply a concerned citizen ready to make a difference, there's a place for you in this movement.

Together, we can accelerate conscious evolution and create a thriving Earth. The future is in our hands, and the time to act is now. Will you join us in shaping the Sophia Century?

Contact Greg:

https://www.linkedin.com/in/greg-apodaca-b115464/

References <source links>

1. Join the most vital debate of our times. Kate Raworth, author of Doughnut Economics https://www.kateraworth.com/doughnut/

2. What's left of this decade may be our last best hope to get it at least partly right. Bill McKibben, author, of The End of Nature https://billmckibben.com/end-of-nature.html

3. This is a roadmap that cannot be ignored. Sharan Burrow, General secretary, International Trade Union Confederation. https://en.wikipedia.org/wiki/Sharan_Burrow

4. An absolute read for policy-makers and leaders. Janez Potoimik, former European Commissioner for Environment, 2990-02014 https://en.wikipedia.org/wiki/Janez_Poto%C4%8Dnik

5. It is an aspirational future, it is livable for all, and most critically it is achievable. Carlota Perez, author, of Technological Revolutions and Financial Capital https://en.wikipedia.org/wiki/Technological_Revolutions_and_Financial_Capital

6. Lynne Twist does a TedX talk on "The Sophia Century," which is defined as the time in our history when the feminine archetype returns, awakening women and men to transform the world. https://youtu.be/iz18RQ7UR3w?feature=shared

7. Empathy In Action is a book trending nextgen in employee experience by Tony Bates and Natalie Petouhoff https://www.amazon.com/Empathy-Action-Tony-Bates/dp/1646870433

8. A call for governments of the world to upgrade their economic systems. A must-read. Jane Kabubo-Mariara, president of, the African Society for Ecological Economics https://basis.ucdavis.edu/people/jane-kabubo-mariara

9. Threading the needle between what is good government and what is good for society is hard. Earth for all https://earth4all.life/ provides a powerful new framework that's a must-read for every impact investor. Doug Heske, Founder, Newday Impact Investing https://newdayimpact.com/

Key References:

1. "Breaking Boundaries" - Netflix documentary with David Attenborough and Johan Rockstrom https://www.netflix.com/title/81336476

2. "Thank You For Being Late" by Thomas Friedman Thank You For Being Late" by Thomas Friedman

3. PSI Seminars and Landmark Education (for personal transformation concepts) https://www.landmarkworldwide.com/ec/schedules?gad_source=1

4. Wharton School of Public Policy paper: "Can the world change course on climate change?" https://lgst.wharton.upenn.edu/profile/bberkey/

5. Salim Ismail's TED Talk: "How to fix civilization" https://youtu.be/mV0oKVOIGG4?feature=shared

6. Lynne Twist's book: "Living A Committed Life" https://www.amazon.com/Living-Committed-Life-Fulfillment-Yourself/dp/1523093099

7. Peter Diamandis and Steven Kotler's book: "The Future Is Faster Than You Think" https://www.amazon.com/Future-Faster-Than-You-Think/dp/1982109661

Powerful Quotes:

1. "What we can do we must do." - Attributed to Salim Ismail

2. "Here's to the crazy ones. The misfits. The rebels. The troublemakers. The round pegs in the square holes. The ones who see things differently. They're not fond of rules. And they have no respect for the status quo. You can quote them, disagree with them, glorify, or vilify them. About the only thing you can't do is ignore them. Because they change things. They push the human race forward. And while some may see them as the crazy ones, we see genius. Because the people who are crazy enough to think they can change the world are the ones who do." - Apple Inc.

3. "Committing to a purpose larger than yourself has the power to not only give your life meaning but to make a difference at a time when humanity faces the greatest challenges we've ever known." - Lynne Twist

Lynne Twist's Amazon Rainforest Vision

In her book "Living A Committed Life," Lynne Twist describes a transformative experience in the Ecuadorean Amazon. During a ceremony led by shaman John Perkins, she had a vision:

"People somewhere are calling to you, and you must go to them," the shaman said. "Lynne, it's the Achuar people deep in the Amazon rainforest. They have been told in their dreams and ceremonies that they need to partner with people who can support them in preserving their land and culture. This is an extraordinary opportunity, and you and I have to respond and go there."

Initially reluctant, Twist eventually felt compelled to return to the Amazon after repeated visions. This calling wasn't just from the Achuar people, but from the rainforest itself, from life, and the future yet to be created.

This story could illustrate the power of committing to a larger purpose and how sometimes our life's mission finds us in unexpected ways.

CHAPTER 6
BEYOND IQ: UNCOVERING HIDDEN TALENTS - A FUTURE RETROSPECTIVE

JONATHAN FROST

Part 1: The Spark of an Idea

In the historic and industrial city of Sheffield, there lived a scientist and teacher named Jon. Known for his innovative teaching methods, Jon had always believed that every individual harbored a unique skill, often undiscovered. He had talked to many teenagers who were considered trouble in the classroom but experts when it came to handling plants and animals in the real world. As time passed he found himself missing the highlights of teaching and yearned to make a difference. One evening, as he browsed through his old teaching training notes about Howard Gardner and his multiple intelligence theory, an idea struck him like a bolt of lightning. What if he could create an online quiz that could uncover people's hidden skills and talents that were missed in the classroom? What if he could bring Gardner's insights of the 1980s into the present?

Howard Gardner's Multiple Intelligences Theory is a revolutionary concept in understanding human cognition and potential. This theory proposes that intelligence is not a single, uniform ability, but rather a combination of several distinct types of intelligence. Gardner initially identified seven intelligences: Linguistic, Logical-Mathematical, Musical, Bodily-Kinaesthetic, Spatial, Interpersonal, and Intrapersonal. Later, he added Naturalistic and, in some interpretations, Existential and Moral intelligences.

Gardner's theory allows individuals to identify their unique combination of intelligence. Understanding these strengths can guide people toward careers that match their innate abilities and passions, leading to more fulfilling and purposeful work. In changing times, rigid career paths are restrictive. Gardner's theory encourages flexibility, suggesting that people can excel in multiple areas. For instance, someone with high interpersonal intelligence might thrive in teaching, counseling, or sales, while someone with strong spatial intelligence could excel in architecture, engineering, or graphic design.

Understanding multiple intelligences helps educational institutions and employers develop more effective training programs. For example, a training program that incorporates musical elements (like rhythm or melody) could be more engaging for someone with high musical intelligence. As automation and AI change the job landscape, many traditional roles will evolve or become obsolete. Gardner's theory can help individuals adapt by identifying alternative intelligence they can develop or pivot toward in their careers.

In a workplace, understanding the diverse intelligences of team members can lead to more effective and harmonious team dynamics. For example, someone with strong interpersonal intelligence might be great in client-facing roles, while someone with high logical-mathematical intelligence could excel in data analysis or strategy development. Jobs aligned with an individual's dominant intelligence are likely to be more satisfying and motivating. This alignment leads to higher job satisfaction, productivity, and longevity in a career.

Part 2: The Creation

Jon, though a bit rusty on computer programming, could see that this was ripe for digitizing in a way that wasn't possible in the 1980s. He enlisted the help of his local IT technician in Sheffield and software developers in India and Ukraine. Together, they began to design a sophisticated, yet user-friendly online test. This test was not just a set of fact-based questions; it was a carefully crafted journey through multiple intelligence assessments, designed to unearth the latent skills and passions of anyone who took it.

Branding and Name Creation: The name "Beyond IQ" was chosen for its appeal and resonance with the platform's objective – to uncover latent skills and talents beyond a standard IQ test that only measures basic logical and language aptitude. The team wanted a brand that spoke directly to the aspirations and potential of their users. The logo, a stylized capitalized IQ surrounding a human silhouette looking into the future, symbolized the illumination of hidden talents. The branding was designed to be approachable, inspiring, and representative of personal growth and discovery.

Intellectual Property Protection: Recognizing the value of their unique methodology and the potential of the AI algorithms, Jon took steps to protect their intellectual property. They had a natural copyright covering the specific contents used in the test. Additionally, they registered the trademark name of "Beyond IQ," ensuring their brand identity was safeguarded.

Business Roadmap: Developing a business roadmap was crucial for their vision. They outlined short-term goals, such as finalizing the test's beta version and launching a basic website, and long-term goals, like expanding the test's features and reaching global markets. This roadmap also included plans for funding, scaling up the technology, and building a team to support various business functions.

Market Research: Before fully launching the test, Jon's team conducted extensive market research. They analyzed current trends in career counseling, online education platforms, and personality assessment tools. This research helped them find gaps in the market landscape, identify their target audience, and position "Beyond IQ" to meet the needs of a diverse user base.

Future Jobs Demand Research: Anticipating the evolving job market, they invested resources in researching future job trends and demands. Many industries are evolving and shifting in response to changing economic and environmental conditions. As resources become scarce, certain careers will grow in importance and demand. These careers generally don't necessitate a full-fledged degree, but instead, prioritize practical experience and specialized training. This research was crucial for ensuring that the test and subsequent career guidance remained relevant and valuable. They collaborated with industry experts, HR professionals, and futurists to gain insights into emerging career fields and skills likely to be in demand in the coming years. They collaborated with the team at MoveableType.ai to produce career-related books like "Thrive in a Changing Economy: Alternative Careers for a Sustainable Future", to act as lead magnets at the top of the marketing funnel.

Part 3: The Launch - Strategic Outsourcing and Marketing Integration

Jon's team knew that the successful launch of "BeyondIQ.uk" would require more than just a functional platform; it needed a comprehensive marketing and operational strategy. They focused on outsourcing key elements, including a marketing funnel, email sequences, and integrating additional services.

Outsourcing Graphic Design: Understanding the importance of a visually appealing platform, they outsourced the graphic design work to a professional agency. This agency helped create a visually compelling website and user interface for the test, ensuring it was not only intuitive but also engaging for users. The design elements extended to marketing materials, like a distinctive logo and social media graphics, maintaining brand consistency.

Funnel Building: Building an effective marketing funnel was crucial for converting visitors into users and clients. They designed a funnel that began with awareness through social media and online ads, leading to interest via informative blog posts and webinars about purposeful career choice, and culminating in decision and action, where visitors would be encouraged to take the test and sign up for additional services. This funnel was optimized continuously based on user feedback and analytics.

Email Sequence Design: A key component of their strategy was the development of a targeted email sequence. Once a user completed the test, they would receive a series of emails tailored to their results. These emails offered further insights, additional resources, and invitations to schedule coaching sessions. The sequence was designed to nurture leads, providing value at each step and gently guiding users towards the coaching services.

Integration with Coaching Booking Systems: The platform was integrated with a coaching booking system, allowing users to easily schedule sessions with career coaches. This integration was seamless, ensuring a smooth transition from the test to booking a session, enhancing user experience, and increasing the likelihood of conversion.

Upsells and Downsells: To maximize revenue and cater to different user needs, Jon's team implemented upsell and downsell strategies. Users interested in deeper, personalized guidance were upsold to one-on-one coaching sessions with a higher price point. For those not ready to commit to coaching, they offered downsell in the form of affordable eBooks and online courses related to career development and self-discovery.

The results were astonishing. A bank teller discovered a talent for graphic design, a stay-at-home mum found out she had a knack for coding, and a high school student realized he had exceptional comedic skills. The success stories began to spread, and "Beyond IQ" quickly gained popularity.

Part 4: Scaling Up with the 6Ds - Digitized, Deceptive, Disruptive, Demonetize, Dematerialize, Democratize

Jon knew he had tapped into something extraordinary. To scale his venture, he turned to the principles of Exponential Organisations (ExOs). he embraced the ExO attributes: a Massive Transformative Purpose (MTP) – "Uncover and Empower Hidden Talents in Everyone." He leveraged technologies like AI to refine the test for different age groups, translate it into multiple languages, and crowdsourced insights from industry experts to enhance the platform's effectiveness.

As "Beyond IQ" began to gain traction, Jon recognized the need to scale his venture rapidly and sustainably. He decided to incorporate three of the six D's, fundamental principles often seen in rapidly growing digital businesses: digitized, deceptive, and disruptive.

Digitized: First, Jon focused on fully digitizing his platform. This meant enhancing the online test with more interactive and dynamic elements. He integrated advanced AI algorithms to analyze responses more deeply, offering more accurate and personalized skill assessments. The platform transitioned from a simple website to a sophisticated, AI-driven engine capable of handling complex data inputs and providing insightful outputs. This digitization allowed "Beyond IQ" to process a vast amount of data efficiently, catering to an ever-growing global user base.

Deceptive: The growth of "Beyond IQ" at this stage seemed modest at first, almost deceptive. Jon and his team faced skepticism; many couldn't fathom how an online test could accurately unearth hidden skills and talents. However, this deception was a phase of underestimation. As the platform's AI became more refined and its database richer, the accuracy and depth of the insights provided by the test improved significantly. What started as a simple online test became a powerful tool, slowly gaining credibility and catching the attention of larger, more influential audiences.

Disruptive: The real turning point for "Beyond IQ" was its disruptive impact. The platform not only provided insights into people's hidden talents but also began offering tailored learning paths and career suggestions based on the test results. This approach disrupted the traditional career counseling and talent management industries. Instead of general advice, "Beyond IQ" offered a highly personalized career development plan, making it a sought-after tool for individuals, educational institutions, and corporations alike. This disruption was felt across various sectors, as it challenged the conventional norms of talent identification and development.

By leveraging these three D's, Jon was able to scale "Beyond IQ" from a simple online test to a global platform that challenged and changed the way people thought about their careers and potential. This growth phase was not just about expanding the user base, but also about fundamentally altering the approach to personal and professional development.

Demonetize: Jon sought to make "Beyond IQ" accessible to a wider audience by reducing the cost barriers. He introduced a freemium model, where the basic test and some fundamental features were free, with more advanced services available for a fee. This strategy demonetized the traditional cost structure of career coaching, making it affordable for a larger demographic. Additionally, he formed partnerships with educational institutions and non-profits, offering discounted rates, thereby further reducing the financial barrier to access.

Dematerialize: The next step was the dematerialization of the platform. Jon and his team worked to ensure that all aspects of the service were available online, eliminating the need for physical resources. This included digitizing learning materials, online coaching sessions, and interactive webinars. By moving everything to a virtual space, "Beyond IQ" not only reduced its environmental footprint but also made its resources more accessible to users regardless of their geographical location.

Democratise: Finally, Jon focused on democratizing the platform. He wanted "Beyond IQ" to be a tool for everyone, not just those who were actively seeking career changes. The platform was made user-friendly to accommodate people of all ages and backgrounds. They also introduced multilingual support, ensuring that language was not a barrier. By democratizing access, "Beyond IQ" became a global platform where anyone, from a student in a remote village to a professional in a bustling city, could discover and harness their hidden skills.

Through these efforts, "Beyond IQ" transcended from being a simple skill-assessment tool to a global platform offering accessible, affordable, and environmentally conscious career development services. Jon's vision of a world where everyone could unlock their potential was becoming a reality, redefining how people approached their careers and personal growth.

Part 5: Global Reach - Implementing ExO Principles for Worldwide Expansion

As "Beyond IQ" grew, Jon's team realized that to achieve a truly global reach, they needed to embrace more Exponential Organization (ExO) principles. The platform, now a hub for career guidance and skill development, attracted global attention. It wasn't just individuals using "Beyond IQ"; corporations began employing it to discover and nurture talent within their teams, schools used it for student career guidance, and governments recognized it as a tool for workforce development. They focused on Interfaces, Dashboards, Experimentation, Autonomy, and Social Technologies to scale their impact worldwide.

Interfaces: To manage the increasing influx of users and data, "Beyond IQ" developed sophisticated interfaces. These interfaces streamlined interactions between the platform and its users, regardless of their location. They ensured that the test and subsequent resources were easily accessible and user-friendly. Additionally, these interfaces facilitated seamless interactions between users and career coaches across different time zones, languages, and cultures.

Dashboards: Data-driven decision-making was crucial for scaling up. Jon's team implemented comprehensive dashboards that provided real-time insights into user engagement, test performance, and user feedback. These dashboards were instrumental in understanding user needs and preferences across different regions, allowing for tailored content and services. This data also helped in identifying emerging career trends globally, keeping "Beyond IQ" ahead of the curve.

Experimentation: Adopting a culture of experimentation, "Beyond IQ" constantly tested new features, marketing strategies, and business models in different markets, including translation into many languages. This approach allowed them to understand what worked and what didn't in various cultural contexts. Experimentation led to innovations in how the test was administered, how results were communicated, and how follow-up services were offered, ensuring relevance and effectiveness in diverse global markets.

Autonomy: To manage their expanding global presence, Jon's team decentralized operations, giving regional teams a degree of autonomy. These teams had the freedom to adapt the platform's offerings to local markets while maintaining the core values and objectives of "Beyond IQ." This autonomy ensured that the platform remained culturally sensitive and relevant, enhancing user experience and satisfaction.

Social Technologies: Recognizing the power of social media and community, "Beyond IQ" leveraged social technologies to build a global community of users, coaches, and career development enthusiasts. They created online forums, social media groups, and virtual events where individuals could share experiences, network, and support each other. This fostered a sense of global community, essential for the platform's organic growth and user engagement.

Part 6: The Premier Career Guide Platform - Widening the Sphere of Influence

"Beyond IQ" transformed into the premier global career guide platform. It became a beacon for those seeking to understand and leverage their skills. Jon's vision had materialized into a global movement, empowering millions to pursue purposeful careers aligned with their newly discovered talents. Its use expanded far beyond individual students, encompassing graduates, employees, employers, universities, and recruitment agencies. This broadening of scope transformed the platform into a comprehensive career development ecosystem.

Students and Graduates: "Beyond IQ" became a fundamental tool for students and recent graduates. High schools and universities incorporated the test into their career counseling programs, helping students identify their strengths and potential career paths early on. For graduates, the platform became a guide in navigating the often overwhelming transition from academia to the workforce, providing insights into careers they might not have considered but were well-suited for.

Employees and Employers: In the corporate world, "Beyond IQ" found a new role. Employees used the test to understand their hidden skills and potential for growth within their current roles. This insight helped them in their personal development and in mapping out their career trajectories within organizations. Employers, on the other hand, utilized the platform for talent management and employee development. It became a tool to identify hidden talents within their workforce, helping to guide training programs and internal promotions.

Universities: Higher education institutions began to use "Beyond IQ" for both career guidance for their students and alumni, and internal staff development. Universities leveraged the test to align their curricula with emerging job market trends, making their programs more relevant and attractive to prospective students.

Recruitment Agencies: Recruitment agencies found "Beyond IQ" invaluable for matching candidates with suitable job roles. The platform's ability to unearth latent talents helped recruiters to place candidates in roles that were not just based on their past experience or education but also on their inherent abilities and potential for growth. This led to more successful job placements and satisfied clients.

The widespread adoption of "Beyond IQ" across these diverse sectors illustrated the universal appeal and effectiveness of the platform. It wasn't just a test; it was a movement that redefined how individuals and organizations approached career development and talent management. "Beyond IQ" has become the go-to solution for anyone looking to discover hidden talents and for any organization seeking to harness the full potential of its human resources.

Epilogue: A Legacy Cemented

Jon, once a simple teacher with a love for discovery, had ignited a global revolution in career development and personal growth. As he sat in his study, reflecting on his journey, his heart swelled with pride, not just for his accomplishments, but for the countless lives transformed by his daring to dream. "Beyond IQ" had become a testament to the power of belief, innovation, and the unrelenting pursuit of uncovering the potential within us all.

Contact: https://www.linkedin.com/in/jonathanfrost62/

Notes

6D's – digitized, deceptive, disruptive, demonetize, dematerialize, and democratize.

'IDEAS' – Interfaces, Dashboards, Experimentation, Autonomy and Social Technologies

'SCALE' – Staff on Demand, Community and Crowd, Algorithms, Leveraged Assets and Engagement.

CHAPTER 7
SYNTROPIC ENTERPRISE PRINCIPLES FOR DUMMIES – A PRIMER FOR A NOVEL ECONOMIC REASONING AND START-UP IMPLEMENTATION CONCEPTS

CHRISTINE MCDOUGALL
Interviewed by Niki Faldemolaei - Michael Friebe, PhD

The SYNTROPIC Principles

The Trust Manifesto is a simple, plain English enterprise agreement and threshold-crossing template, outlining the purpose, Pattern Integrity, and Source Idea of the enterprise, plus the conditions of engagement that ensure ecologies of synergy become normal. This might include how people respond and behave with each other, how conflict is managed, who controls or decides what, when, where, and how, how the money is handled, and what leadership looks like. Each Trust manifesto is bespoke to the enterprise. It is a living document, as all things in Syntropic Enterprises are living systems.

A healthy Trust Manifesto means the ecology of the enterprise is healthy. A diverse group of people collaborate synergistically.

Without a Trust Manifesto, there is no threshold-crossing boundary, and people will behave and respond as they like when they like. The usual consequence is a messy human heap, where the disfunction of humans becomes more energetically demanding than the ability to attend to the purpose around which the humans have gathered.

The Synergistic Audit is a process of accounting for multiple domains of value existing in dynamic polarity.

It ensures that one domain of value, such as money, never holds primacy over all other domains of value.

When the Synergistic Audit is used in all relational dynamics, it enables an all-in-accounting of both measurable and immeasurable qualities, values, inputs, and outputs.

The Synergistic Audit, therefore, is recommended to be used as the threshold crossing of all relationships. Recruitment, project work, provisioning and funding, partnering agreements, and community engagements.

The Steward Leader takes the role of steward or guardian (even gestating parent) of the Source Idea and its Pattern Integrity. Their role is to ensure the Pattern Integrity is never violated. They are responsible for attunement to the inner and outer ecology and environment of the enterprise, making adjustments as needed based on changing and emergent conditions. They have an intimate and communing relationship with the Source Idea and Pattern Integrity, seeking to enable its fullest and healthiest expression. (As a parent to a child and their unique expression.)

Q&A:

Yes, I align with these ideas and concepts ... but the world around me is not ready! What would you recommend on how to start a new venture based on synthetic-based principles? What is the minimum requirement?

The minimum requirements are clarity around the Evolutionary Purpose, Source Idea, and Pattern Integrity, the application of a Trust Manifesto equivalent, and the practice of the Synergistic Audit. Then, be sure not to replicate any code of domination, patriarchy, superiority, imperialism, or exploitation of people as a starting point. Be the model in all things of the world you are working to create.

Could you provide any ideas on how to market these principles as part of the start-up activities? An easy and fast way — e.g. elevator pitch — that allows us to communicate the difference between a SYNTROPIC and conventional Enterprise?

This is actually exceedingly simple, yet hard to arrive at. When we have the core elements, Evolutionary Purpose, Source Idea, and Pattern Integrity, and we have the enterprise architecture (Trust Manifesto and Synergistic Audit) in place, and we have considered deeply the precessional effects (side effects) of our source idea becoming manifest, our words and self become a transmission.

Like any elevator pitch or pitch, arriving at this level of clarity is the work. Most startups fail at this. They do not get funded or supported because they have not done the hard design work.

A Syntropic Enterprise is integrity in practice. Sometimes, this is fast and easy, but mostly, this requires deep work. Syntropy does not aspire to be fast and easy. It seeks integrity first and foremost.

Can you provide a visual overview of the concepts and artifacts that are associated with SYNTROPY?

How to start a Syntropic Enterprise.

Can you provide a guideline and maybe a timeline of implementation steps, considering the balance between building and securing a business and convincing external stakeholders, as well as regular syntropic and synergistic accounting steps?

Syntropic Enterprises adopts the Cathedral building premise: Building something beautiful and enduring that truly serves humanity and life is not a rush job. To go fast, slow down. We practice Kairos time - which is the clock of the heavens, like cycles and seasons. Nature has its own gestation rate. Only humans seek to force everything into linear, predictable time. Anyone who has ever built a business will tell you that forcing strategy onto something is to ignore what is revealed when we take the next step. Everything has changed. The better question might be, how are you living on the edge of emergence and listening to what is needed? The emergent strategy is Syntropic.

What would you recommend a start-up in the tech-space (e.g. the healthcare space) to do to become a SYNTROPIC Enterprise?

The same as I would say to any startup. Get the foundations in place. This is the work that happens before we see anything above ground. Foundations are key. Upon a great foundation, we can build anything. As above - Source Idea, pattern integrity, evolutionary purpose, Trust Manifesto, Synergistic Audit, plus the legal codes that are in integrity to your unique purpose. Consider the precession. The accelerated growth happens after the foundations are there. Growth without foundations will fail.

We are living in an exponentially fast-changing time with disruptive technologies that open up new opportunities but also might lead to economic chaos and uncertainty. How can SYNTROPIC help or provide guidance?

To begin, start with questioning the model of speed. The technology we have comes now with grave existential danger to all life.

Admit if you want to be on the train at speed no matter what, or, if you want to lead through the tunnel of chaos and remain resilient and enduring while others around you burn. They are two very different strategies. A Syntropic Strategy is towards life for all. You do not rush this. But like the tortoise and the hare, you may well be the one left standing.

Where can I get more information?
Https://syntropic.world

Some Requirements and To-Do's

Applying the Syntropic Enterprise principles to your startup business involves a shift in mindset and operational practices and for that, you need to address the following aspects:

Purpose and Vision:

Clarify your business's purpose beyond profit. What positive impact do you want to create for people, the environment, and society?

Develop a vision that aligns with the sacredness of life and interconnectedness.

Stakeholder Mapping:

Identify all stakeholders: employees, customers, suppliers, communities, and ecosystems.

Understand their needs, aspirations, and well-being.

Collaboration and Synergy:

Foster collaboration within your organization and with external partners.
Seek win-win solutions rather than zero-sum competition.

Leadership and Stewardship:

As a leader, act as a steward of the enterprise.
Facilitate synergy, encourage learning, and empower others.

All-In Accounting:

Go beyond financial accounting. Consider the impact on all stakeholders.
Measure success in terms of well-being, vitality, and equity.

Integrity and Alignment:

Ensure your actions align with the principles.
Communicate transparently and authentically.

Regenerative Practices:

Implement practices that regenerate ecosystems, communities, and relationships.
Reduce waste, promote a circular economy, and prioritize regenerative resources.

1. What are Syntropic Principles?

All Syntropic Principles are found in Nature's law and coordinate system. They are true in all cases on planet Earth and, as such, should be found in both Indigenous and wisdom traditions.

Humanity has deemed it acceptable to design enterprises, institutions, education, monetary, financial, banking, housing, energy, legal, and accounting systems that do not use the codes and laws of Nature. As such, they keep human life and human systems separate from Nature. Given humans are Nature, we have constructed systems that have us separate from ourselves, each other, and the things that matter most.

Nature's coordinate system is intimately relational. The quality and integrity of the relational field enable flourishing. When our relational field is unhealthy, including our relationship with self and Earth and her creatures, ill health becomes systemic.

The Principle of principles is Synergy = the behavior of the whole system cannot be determined by an examination of the parts separately. The practice of this principle means we must look to the whole first. (This is a systems view incorporating complexity.)

Some other principles include. (There are many)

Precession - to any body in motion there is an effect, at 90 degrees to the body in motion.
Unity is plural at minimum two. Existence requires polarity.
Integrity = to hold its shape. Oneness.

In addition to the application of Syntropic Principles, the Pattern Integrity of the Source Idea of the Syntropic World includes holding the sacredness of all life as the central organizing principle of all actions, Synergistic Accounting = all-in-accounting, zero exploitation, extraction to extinction and imperialism, the leader as steward, natural rather than dominator hierarchies, and profit as a precessional effect.

References. Critical Path. R.Buckminster Fuller
https://www.amazon.com/Critical-Path-Kiyoshi-Kuromiya/dp/0312174918

A Fuller Explanation - Amy Edmondson
https://www.amazon.com/Fuller-Explanation-Buckminster-Back-Action-ebook/dp/B002YQ2X5S/

2. Why syntropy is needed now?

Our world operating system is designed to do exactly what it is doing.

1. Increasing the divide between those with wealth and power and those without.
2. Amplification of climate change
3. Increased commodification of all things.
4. Endless need for growth to keep the system alive
5. An amplification of fear, division, racism, and caste systems in every shape and form, including intellectual and economic.
6. A continued expression of domination, patriarchy, superiority, and imperialism, winner takes all.
7. The decimation of species, including species of people.
8. The rise of the extreme right, fascism and oligarchy.

We need a new operating system. One that places the sacredness of life as central to all actions and incentives.

We can no longer seek to change the existing operating system and expect a different result. The attempt to change the existing system fails every time.

Syntropy is the new operating system designed in partnership with Nature.

References.

Less is More - how degrowth will save the world Jason Hickel –

https://www.amazon.com/Less-More-Degrowth-Will-World/dp/B08DL4GXRN/

Cory Doctorow - Pluralistic. https://pluralistic.net/

Planet Critical Rachel Donald Substack
https://www.planetcritical.com/

Brett Scott - CloudMoney - Cash, cards, and crypto and the war for our wallets. https://www.amazon.com/Cloudmoney-Cash-Cards-Crypto-Wallets/dp/006293631X

3. More on how to start a syntropic enterprise

Syntropic World offers this in a PDF.

Formation of teams - before governance/entity choice

Any change humans urgently need requires human coordination. The major changes are systemic and global. Climate change cannot be changed by one nation or group. It requires all-human coordination and collaboration. The big question is, given the diversity of people, their world views, and desires, how do we bring diverse people together to work on these major issues and do so in a way that enables collaboration with diversity?

This is to create human syntropic enterprising, which is a design science deeply rooted in the skills and tools of the Syntropic World.

When we have the design right, the people can bring their unique agency to the collective and work collaboratively.

There is a need for support and facilitation with advanced and nuanced communication, such as that provided in the Dare to Care workshop.

Decolonization

Why women, first nations, unlikely allies, underserved? Why now?

Our current operating system is one with embedded coding and behavior that supports domination, white supremacy, patriarchy, imperialism, racism, and superiority.

We will not survive unless this changes.

Any natural healthy system has polarity built in by design.

When we eradicate the polarity, the yin to the yang, we create a highly unstable, unhealthy system. Which is what we have.

Until the decision-making tables in all domains are representative of the human family, we will continue to remain unhealthy.

The most affected by the egregious misuse of power and control by white males often have the most practical solutions to the issues they face on the ground.

Indigenous wisdom from cultures that survived and thrived for 40,000 or more years has something of huge significance to offer those of us who have deemed ourselves superior and, in our superiority, have applied systems and structures that are entropic and anti-nature.

- feminine/masculine archetypes in nature, why not societies

As above. Our operating system is man-made and dissonant with every design principle of Nature.

- how the industrial age is ruining the climate by imposing human build-outs

To answer, this goes beyond the Industrial Age.

As Amitav Ghosh writes in The Nutmeg's Curse: Parables for a Planet in Crisis https://www.amazon.com/Nutmegs-Curse-Parables-Planet-Crisis/dp/0226815455 - the Western human desire to conquer lands, known as colonization and imperialism, has literally terraformed the earth. And continues to do so.

The insatiable desire for domination over Earth, her creatures, and all life is relentless and unsustainable.

Colonization, imperialism, and capitalism are all entwined with the same codes and generator functions. They are the core substrate of human civilization today. The water to us as the fish. To even begin to think we can solve climate change without addressing these issues is to be delusional. In our haste to profit at all costs, we do not consider the precessional (side effects) of our terraforming of the land. Cutting. Digging. Exterminating. The consequences are dire. Beyond soil becoming absent any nutrients, we have erosion, flooding, sea level rise, fires, toxic rivers and oceans, dead reefs, and poisoned air and water. Every single drop of water on the planet today has PFAS chemicals in it. https://www.bbc.com/news/science-environment-62391069

Those people who have contributed the least to this are the most affected.

The global north has and continues to scrape its wealth from the Global South, leaving terrible destruction and poverty, increasing the need for humans to seek refuge in other countries.

The IPCC report states that By one estimate, between 31 million and 72 million people across sub-Saharan Africa, South Asia, and Latin America would be displaced by 2050 due to water stress, sea level rise, and crop failure, even under an aggressive effort to cut global emissions.

The tragedy is that humanity is trapped in the Molochian game theory, which goes like this: If you have nuclear weapons, then we need nuclear weapons because we do not know how many nuclear weapons you have. If you cut down all the forests to profit, then we need to cut down all the forests to also profit because unless we do, we will lose the game of profit. If you have powerful AI, we need powerful AI so you cannot dominate. Never enough. Always from fear. The code is to dominate, win, extract, exploit, enslave, dehumanize.

Any code or operating system that perpetuates these functions must end and be replaced with functions to regenerate, synergize, humanize, connect, commune, love, respect, and revere. This is to be Syntropic.

- language, the origin of words, changing up how we raise kids and future stewards; from fairy tales & organized religion to historical records.

Language, myth, and story create culture. Change language, myth, and story and we change culture. When we have a culture that lives in fear, scarcity, original sin (%$#!!), domination, supremacy, and imperialism, then we need to change the myths and stories, including the historical record of what humans have done to each other. We must confront our terrible truth, the cruelty imposed on millions of people, eradicating 90% of populations and cultures. This is the work of the Awakenings Workshop, now part of the Syntropic collection - with Cindy Forde and I.

The discipline of going to Source to understand the Pattern integrity - the code built into the Source Idea of all things - is a necessary practice for those seeking to steward a healthy and viable future for Earth and all her creatures.

Exploitation

1% dominance (survival, migrants, unemployment, covid exploiting self-employed, freemium models)

Exploitation is integral to our current operating system. Capitalism requires either cheaper labor or cheaper goods. For capitalism to survive, this next year alone, it needs to create an extra amount of capital equal to the entire GDP of Great Britain. Given that this growth imperative is annually exponential, we are not far from a capital growth requirement beyond the GDP of the entire planet.

A young child knows that endless growth on a finite planet is impossible in maths. Mars won't cut it.

Our migrant problem is also going to become an exponential growth curve as more and more people on the margins are forced off their land and homes because of Climate change and war.

Jason Hickel is the better reference to this.

We live in a world where migrating out of the periphery to escape imperial plunder is a crime, but systematically plundering the periphery is considered perfectly normal and legitimate. Jason Hickel

I wrote today's Beauty of Beginnings blog about free.

Why do I object to the use of the word free?

In truth Nature's bounty gifted life to all creatures.

Most creatures take what they need and leave the rest. When this happens, abundance is normal.

Humans take more than they need, ravaging the earth and decimating forests. They abuse the gift.

When we assume something is free, we debase its intrinsic value. For there is always value to be found, expressed in multiple domains. The entanglement of money as the arbiter of value is insidious.

This is free and becomes a seduction to the ongoing illusion of no value.

Instead, this has no monetary fee attached stating that only the value assigned to money is missing.

When we state that the sunlight is free, we debase the gift of the sun. It is gifted, which is not the same as free.

Language matters.

Your work and time are not free. Ever. When we participate in this charade, we participate in a story about exploitation. We sanction exploitation.

Instead, negotiate an exchange that honors and respects the value of the gift.

Free of monetary price invites a different exchange. Be sure to name clearly what that exchange is.

Capitalism

Capitalism has as its Pattern Integrity, the following key features.

Capital is king. Capital requires either cheaper labor or cheaper raw materials. It seeks to commodify everything, including now, water, land, and nature's rights, estimated to be the biggest gain for Wall Street than any other bounty.

(See below from Beauty of Beginnings also this week on the commodification of the commons.)

Capital needs to make a profit of money. At any cost. As such it dehumanises. It cares naught for the land, the future (except one where capitalism lives) of health and vitality. It profits from ill-health, death, poverty, low wages, exploitation, imperialism.

Privatisation and the commons

The commons - At the minimum, our air, water, forests, oceans. Shared assets are essential to all life thriving.

To even think that any of these assets can be privatized is to conflate the impossible.

Private and commons are mutually exclusive. The words themselves are an impossible math. You can have one, not both. Commons. Or private.

Yet our operating system loves the myth of privatization. That somehow when we make a commons a private asset, everyone will gain.

This myth is the central thesis of the neoliberal story.

That privatization is the best way to go. Better management, they say, as if the public are unable to manage things. Tell that to a culture that managed things well for 65,000 years.

The intent behind privatization is more profit. The intent behind a healthy commons is to create an asset for everyone. The two intentions combined end in a negative number. This is entropic.

When we live in a world that insists on profit in all things as the measure of success and health, we have chosen the path that consumes everything.

- inflation, deflation, compounding interest

Show me a compounding interest in nature. Nature does not do monopoly. When a colony of bacteria takes over everything, nature recalibrates it. Cancer will kill then host if it is allowed to. Only humans have a monopoly. Compounding interest is a form of monopoly.

Our dollar's buying power is decreased in inflation. The house price did not go up. The exchange of your dollars has gone down. It is a false illusion. Human-constructed monetary systems are not isomorphic with natural design. (We are nature, so our system is anti-life.)

- future of DeFi and ReFi

It is just capitalism trying to reinvent itself in a new costume to propagate the illusion of its viability. The internal structure may have changed, but it still operates in the current operating system and substrate. If you question this, consider who has the power, what the incentive is, how you will know it has been successful, who is creating it (Men? women? Black people? Institutions already in power), and who is funding it. (Those already in power?)

Please read Cory Doctorow on this topic, plus the topics of AI.

- traditional finance attempting to centralize crypto

As above the big banks and finance institutions getting on the gravy train for short-term gain while they prop up the illusion of capitalism's viability.

Contact Christine

My LinkedIn https://www.linkedin.com/in/christinemcdougall/ also gives access to the full report on Big Blue Sky Case study.

My insight article on this topic:
https://insight.openexo.com/natures-universal-code-applying-syntropic-principles-to-regenerate-our-future/

CHAPTER 8
THE EXO SPECTRUM:
FROM GIANTS TO NIMBLE STARTUPS
(AND EVERYTHING IN-BETWEEN)

Huba Rostonics

Enabling the 99.9% to Thrive by helping young organizations construct the scaffolding to continue to build

When we talk about Exponential Organization (ExO) transformations, the stories that often grab the headlines are about big enterprises or unicorn startups. These work great for showing the massive potential of ExO transformations, mainly because they're well-known organizations, and their success stories tend to be huge. But here's the thing—they might give the impression that ExO transformations are only for these large, iconic companies. I'm here to tell you that's not the case.

In this chapter, I'll attempt to show you why ExO is for everyone, regardless of size. Here are the key points:

ExO is for all sizes of organizations

- Every ExO transformation will face obstacles, but the challenges will differ based on the organization's size.
- While large organizations struggle with the "corporate immune system", Small and medium businesses often struggle with structure, processes, and resources.
- These challenges can be overcome by implementing a Management Framework, like the System & Soul

framework, to create structure, establish processes, and free up resources.

We will explore the challenges of implementing ExO attributes across different organizational sizes. We'll dive into the unique hurdles and opportunities that large enterprises and small businesses each face on their path to becoming Exponential Organizations. Plus, we'll highlight practical strategies and frameworks that can help smaller organizations navigate this transformation effectively.

Let's go!

The 99.9%

According to the U.S. Chamber of Commerce, there are 33.2 million small businesses, which combined, account for 99.9% of all businesses in the U.S. They are credited with almost two-thirds (63%) of new jobs created. Even if these figures were ten times smaller, Exponential Organization's transformation would still be largely absent among small businesses.

Transforming into an Exponential Organization is not a privilege of the large Enterprise though. Organizations of all sizes can gain from embracing the principles of Exponential Organizations, and in today's rapidly evolving landscape, transforming into an ExO has become a necessity for survival and growth. Traditional business models are being disrupted at an unprecedented pace, and companies that fail to adapt risk being left behind. The need to embrace innovation and scale appropriately while remaining agile is more critical than ever.

Whether you are steering a corporate giant with established processes and significant market presence, a nimble startup with the flexibility to pivot quickly, or everything in-between, the principles of ExO offer a roadmap to sustained success. However, any significant change project will meet challenges, regardless of the environment in which it is brought forward, and size is not necessarily a determinant of fit. The specific issues may look very different, but the result looks very similar: Lackluster success in the best of cases. Let's look into why.

What makes ExO initiatives fail?

By understanding the distinct paths to innovation for both giants and nimble startups, we can uncover tailored approaches that leverage the strengths of each. Ultimately, this chapter aims to equip you with some insights to better decide on how to lead your organization through an ExO transformation, setting you up to thrive in the age of exponential change.

Big organization, big #FAIL

Large organizations, perhaps for their visibility, have been the first to benefit from ExO transformations. They can often dedicate extensive resources, and they have established processes and significant market influence. However, these advantages can also lead to considerable inertia. The sheer size and complexity of large corporations can make it challenging to pivot quickly in response to market shifts or disruptive technologies. For instance, when a new technological advancement emerges, large organizations may take longer to adopt it due to the need for comprehensive evaluations, stakeholder buy-in, and system-wide integrations. Bureaucratic layers and ingrained resistance to change can slow down decision-making and stifle innovation. This scenario is amply described in Exponential Organizations 2.0 and identified as the "corporate immune system". This delay can result in missed opportunities and a competitive disadvantage.

Another common characteristic of large organizations is the difficulty in accessing top leadership. Multiple management layers often separate frontline employees from executive decision-makers, creating communication barriers -sometimes on purpose- that can hinder the flow of innovative ideas. In addition to this, driving ExO transformation may imply changing the behavior of thousands of people, which can be a challenge in itself because of its scale.

A small organization, still as big #FAIL

In contrast, small businesses thrive on their agility. With fewer bureaucratic hurdles and closer-knit teams, smaller organizations can make swift decisions and adapt rapidly to changing market conditions. Communication is more streamlined, and innovative ideas can be implemented without extensive delays. Famously, startups iterate on their product based on customer feedback, allowing them to stay ahead of the innovation curve and respond to emerging trends with greater speed and efficiency.

Also, with fewer hierarchical barriers, employees can communicate directly with founders and top executives, fostering a culture of transparency and rapid decision-making. This direct access to leadership is a powerful enabler of innovation, as ideas can be quickly evaluated and implemented. This nimbleness and level of accessibility can be significant advantages to accelerate the innovation process.

My own #FAIL

In my professional experience, I have been in both camps. In my career, I have implemented "Channel Programs", something very prevalent within the technology industry and what I like to call "the original Staff on Demand". While many large organizations often use direct sales, Channel Programs leverage external partners to sell products or services on behalf of the company, without the need for direct hires. Instead of having the company's sales team engage directly with customers, the organization can tap into a network of hundreds of independent sales agents, distributors, and resellers, enhancing the organization's market reach, scalability, and flexibility.

Working through partners allows organizations to maintain a lean internal team while scaling operations efficiently. Hence the connection with the "staff on demand" ExO attribute. I am well aware of the differences, and I am happy to debate with anyone about them, but it is not the goal of this piece at the moment.

In one particular case at a $750M company, even when they could attribute at least 15% of their revenues to channel partners, it took me almost five years to promote these ideas until they finally named a VP of Channel, elevating the role to an executive level, only to abandon the bold move -once the markets turned sour- a year later. I lost track after that, but SG&A, or Selling, General, and Administrative Expenses, are a good proxy to measure Direct vs. Indirect sales models (assuming a lower cost of sales for Indirect Sales), and they have been consistently around 39%-40% for the last decade.

It took another eight years for the same company to have someone recognized as a channel leader by the prestigious CRN "Women in the Channel" award.

In another opportunity, I joined a $3B company with a heritage of selling directly to a handful of very large clients. They wanted (at least, that's what I was told!) to do business with a more diverse set of customers, through partners. The company was probably on its third or fourth attempt, and I led myself to believe that "this time was different". Eventually, when there was a business downturn, the company scaled down resources and funding from partner-led initiatives. Four years later, the company continues to report the same 11% of its revenues coming from non-traditional, partner-driven markets.

Why? In both of these cases, I attribute the results to the fact that their top leadership had a background in direct sales and were never really convinced about the effectiveness of the alternative model, and also because many powerful direct salespeople felt that these ideas jeopardized their standing in the corporate ladder.

By contrast, at smaller organizations, with the leader on-board, changes can be made quickly, and pulling off any similar political shenanigans is much more difficult without promptly being put in evidence.

However, smaller organizations face different challenges in their ExO transformations. Small businesses are often in the early stages of the Information-Formation-Transformation model or the Forming-Storming-Norming stages of team development. These stages involve a lot of foundational work, team alignment, and process development, which can make it difficult to "land" ExO attributes effectively. The lack of established structures and processes can lead to resource constraints and focus issues, making it challenging for small organizations to integrate new business models and ensure they stick. Despite these hurdles, the inherent agility and close-knit nature of small teams provide a fertile ground for rapid adaptation and innovation once these foundational stages are adequately addressed.

The real challenge with smaller organizations is the degree of dysfunction that can cause the lack of existing processes and systems. Personally, in my work with startups, I have experienced situations where a well-intentioned founder has the inspiration to introduce an ExO attribute, without creating the mechanisms inside the organization to effectively benefit from the attributes.

Some years ago, I was a founding member of Ralentage, Inc (like in "ralentize (slow down) age", but pronounced as it would be French, like "fromage"), where we were developing assistive technologies in support of the families and caregiver teams of dementia patients. We were using mobile networks, wearable devices and IoT, Cloud technologies, and Machine Learning; and the plan was to integrate Dashboards, Interfaces, Algorithms, Staff on Demand, Community, and Crowd. Being an ExO will not shield you from the regular issues of being in business. Ultimately, it was not because of our inability to get these technologies or attributes off the ground that we failed, but for the simplest reason -and the most common one- that startups fail: a disagreement among shareholders.

More recently, I collaborated with the founder of an on-demand live medical translation service. In the business model, Interfaces and Staff on Demand were prevalent. The company offered live translation services over telephone and videoconference, at the touch of a button. As soon as a medical provider required translation services for appropriately servicing a patient, a human translator would be summoned from a pool of translators available, and a connection established. A sort of "Uber for simultaneous translation". The service worked (the ExO piece!) and was delivering value to the customers. However, because there was a lack of attention to basic business elements like understanding the economic engine, nonexistent KPIs, and disregard for the financial side of things, never allowed the organization to scale, and they eventually folded. But the biggest issue was probably that the founder wasn't coachable. While the issues and priorities were clear, they continually defaulted to the same behavior that got them in trouble in the first place.

One recurrent point of contention was related to fixing the existing issues by using external funding. The naked truth is that no investor would risk their capital for a dysfunctional business.

But, is there a way to assess the maturity of an organization, and whether it's ready for a more significant ExO transformation effort?

A Checklist for ExO transformation

Despite the differences in size and structure, both large organizations and small businesses share several critical commonalities when it comes to successfully implementing ExO attributes. These commonalities form the foundation upon which any organization can build an effective transformation strategy.

Leadership Support

Leadership is essential for success. Executive support is crucial for any significant transformation, whether in a large corporation or a small startup. Leaders set the vision, allocate resources, and create a culture that embraces change and innovation. Without strong leadership backing, even the most well-conceived ExO initiatives are likely to falter.

Obtaining leadership support in a large organization can be challenging due to multiple layers of management and entrenched interests. Effective communication from leadership about the importance and benefits of ExO transformation can help overcome resistance and align the entire organization toward common goals. In small businesses, leaders are often directly involved in daily operations and decision-making. This close involvement can accelerate the adoption of ExO principles as leaders can quickly champion new initiatives and inspire their teams, but leaders must remain focused on the ExO vision while navigating the demands of running the day-to-day operations. However, once top leaders are committed, their influence can drive change across the organization.

Staying Power

Any major transformation, particularly one that involves significant experimentation and innovation, will require sustained effort, patience, and resilience over time. The process of embedding new practices, technologies, and cultural shifts into an organization often encounters setbacks and challenges. Leaders must remain committed to the long-term vision, continually driving the transformation forward despite obstacles.

This commitment includes investment, regular communication, and leadership. Successful transformations hinge on the organization's ability to persistently pursue its goals, adapt to emerging insights, and steadily build momentum. This is especially true in the realm of ExO transformation and is captured in Exponential Organizations 2.0 as "Deception", which describes a feature of exponentials where progress appears slow and linear at first, and is often underestimated, or even considered a failure, only to be surprised later by the "hockey stick."

Catalysts for Change

External disruptions, such as technological advancements, market shifts, and competitive pressures, act as catalysts of change for organizations to adopt ExO attributes and should not be underestimated. These disruptions force businesses to reevaluate their strategies and seek innovative solutions to stay relevant and competitive.

Large organizations often face significant disruption from nimble startups and technological innovations that can quickly render established business models obsolete; while small businesses are typically more vulnerable to external disruptions due to their limited resources. However, for the later, their agility allows them to pivot quickly in response to these changes.

While external disruptions are well-known catalysts for change, internal factors can also play a significant role in urging transformation within an organization. One example can be the evolution of leadership. When new leaders take the helm, they often bring fresh perspectives and innovative ideas that can rejuvenate the organization's strategic direction and operational focus. The same can be said about a leader planning to retire, or to pass on the post to someone else.

Other powerful internal catalysts are organizational and process restructuring, cultural shifts, and even the implementation of new technologies and systems.

By re-evaluating and optimizing organizational structures, businesses can improve efficiency, foster better communication, and create a more agile environment. This restructuring often leads to the elimination of silos, encouraging cross-functional collaboration and innovation.

Cultural shifts within the organization can also drive significant change. Lastly, investing in automation tools, data analytics, or new machinery or software platforms can streamline operations, provide better insights, and ultimately drive better decision-making and growth, but they usually require re-thinking how work is performed.

The existence of any type of catalyst of change can be a good indicator, if not for straight-out success, for commitment to the process of change. While other factors provide answers to "Why this?" and "Why us?", a catalyst for change speaks loudly about "Why now?"

Change Management Processes

Both large and small organizations can benefit from having established processes for driving change and continuous improvement. These processes provide a structured approach to implementing ExO attributes, ensuring that initiatives are systematically planned, executed, and refined. Many large organizations have established processes such as Lean Six Sigma, Agile, and continuous improvement programs that provide a solid foundation for implementing ExO principles. These methodologies help large enterprises manage complexity, reduce inefficiencies, and foster a culture of continuous innovation. Integrating ExO attributes into these existing frameworks can enhance their effectiveness and drive exponential growth. In the case of younger, smaller organizations, they may have not yet formalized processes for change management, but they often have a culture of experimentation and iteration. By adopting structured approaches such as a Business Operating Framework, small businesses can create a more disciplined environment for driving ExO transformation.

Turn-Key Business Operating Frameworks

Business Operating Frameworks help small businesses create a structure of responsibilities, measure progress, create recurring events to conduct reviews and prioritize actions to achieve the organization's goals.

Small businesses thrive on their agility, allowing them to pivot quickly and implement changes without the delays seen in larger organizations. This ability to make swift decisions and adapt rapidly to customer feedback, market trends, and technological advancements keeps them at the forefront of innovation. Streamlined communication in small businesses, due to fewer hierarchical layers, fosters a collaborative environment where ideas can flow freely and be quickly implemented, accelerating the innovation process. Additionally, the accessibility of leaders in small organizations enables direct involvement in daily operations, inspiring and motivating teams, championing new initiatives, and making swift decisions that drive transformation and continuous improvement. However, the operational demands, and in some cases even the day-to-day chaos, can consume their time, making it challenging to focus on long-term strategic initiatives without deliberate effort and prioritization.

To address this challenge, implementing a structured framework, like the one illustrated, can help small businesses gain clarity and control.

This framework emphasizes foundational elements such as business purpose, values, and culture, which set the stage for strategic alignment and operational effectiveness. By clearly defining the organization's Massive Transformative Purpose (MTP), vision, and mission, leaders can ensure that every action taken aligns with the overarching goals of the business.

Day-to-day operations are streamlined and supported through robust organizational structures, processes, performance management systems, communication, and collaboration tools; and performance can be objectively measured by key performance indicators (KPIs). These elements ensure that the business runs smoothly and efficiently, even amidst high volumes of daily activities, requiring less involvement from top leadership to keep these functions operating.

A framework like this creates structure and processes and frees up resources, enabling leaders to work ON the business rather than getting bogged down IN the business, facilitating a proactive approach to innovation and transformation.

When this is achieved, higher-level processes like feedback and improvement loops, decision-making protocols, risk and change management, strategy development, governance, and policy setting can provide even more structure for continuous growth and adaptability. This approach helps leaders focus on long-term goals and ensures that the organization is well-prepared to navigate the complexities of exponential transformation and the growth that comes from it.

Building the plane while flying it

This is not to say that organizations cannot take an ExO-inspired approach before they possess a sound operating framework, but more so to understand that not all issues in an organization's aim, strategy, and day-to-day management can be fixed by adopting a subset of the 11 ExO attributes. Dozens of management practices are time-proven, and still relevant in today's business environment, and that will help the organization advance in its journey.

Once a management framework has been identified, it is possible to map the desired ExO attributes that are expected to produce the most return, to elements of the management framework that would support them. Implementing those rapidly can further accelerate the implementation of the ExO attributes. In this sense, and in sort of an ironic fashion ExO transformations are by themselves, an exponential process.

How S2 can support ExO

The table below aims to bridge the gap by mapping key ExO attributes to elements of a Business Operating Framework and facilitating this transformation. By preparing some basic business framework elements, businesses can more effectively implement ExO principles and achieve their transformation goals. The table shows how implementing elements of a specific framework, System & Soul (S2), can help implement related ExO attributes.

ExO Attribute	Supported by (S2)	Implementation Support
Massive Transformative Purpose (MTP)	Understand your Destination, Values, Unique Differentiators	Aligning the organization's overarching goals with ExO's MTP to inspire and drive innovation.
Leverage Staff on Demand	Organizational Structure, Key Internal Processes, Policies, and Decision Trees. Unique Differentiators. Economic Engine.	Creating flexible structures that enable the efficient integration of external talent and resources.
Community & Crowd	Economic Engine. Understand your Destination, Values, and Unique Differentiators. Cadence.	Leveraging collaborative platforms to engage with external communities and harness collective intelligence.
Maximize Business Opportunities with Algorithms	Organizational Structure, Key Internal Processes, Policies, and Decision Trees. Unique Differentiators. Economic Engine.	Utilizing data-driven performance metrics to optimize operations and decision-making.

Used Leveraged Assets	Internal Processes. Unique Differentiators. Economic Engine.	Identifying and managing external assets to minimize risk and enhance scalability.
Engagement	Economic Engine. Understand your Destination, Values, and Unique Differentiators.	Fostering a culture of engagement through shared values and purpose, enhancing employee and stakeholder commitment.
Communicate with Customers via Interfaces	Organizational Structure, Key Customer-Facing Processes	Establishing clear and efficient interfaces for interaction with both internal and external stakeholders.
Create/Utilize Dashboards	Organizational Structure, Key Performance Indicators	Implementing comprehensive dashboards to track performance and make informed decisions.

Experimentation	Key Performance Indicators, Weekly Cadence	Encouraging a culture of continuous experimentation and learning to drive innovation, while still staying in-control.
Grant Autonomy to each group	Destination, Values, Organizational Structure, Key Performance Indicators	Empowering teams and individuals with the autonomy to make decisions and act swiftly.
Social Technologies	Economic Engine. Understand your Destination, Values, and Unique Differentiators.	Utilizing social technologies to enhance collaboration, communication, and information sharing across the organization.

The System & Soul framework is particularly well-suited to be implemented in conjunction with ExO because:

- It allows for bringing in "best in class" tools and practices when they are a fit. System & Soul implementations are not an "all or nothing" proposition.

- It is flexible. Some of the elements of S2 can be adapted to work in conjunction with other frameworks. S2 places a large amount of discretion on the coach to shape how the framework is implemented.

- It emphasizes the drivers of the organization, the destination, values, and culture (the Soul of the organization) which are an important component of ExO as well, as reflected by the Massive Transformative Purpose and how it is communicated. Having a strong culture and alignment around the values and the ultimate purpose of the organization can be helpful to have an entire organization understand the magnitude and the importance of an ExO transformation and driving change during though times.

In extreme cases, organizations that lack a management framework can be chaotic, reactive, and with results that are not consistent, nor repeatable. In an environment like this, the leadership is constantly overworked, and reacting to crises to be able to deal with the work. The less-than-ideal results frequently also mean that resources are not available to reinvest in new initiatives. For an ExO transformation to be effective, and even possible, this dysfunction must be dealt with. After all, the saying goes "flying the plane while building it", not addressing the dysfunction would be like ignoring the whole "while building" part, and just "flying", with no plane.

Playing to the organization's strengths

When embarking on an ExO transformation, it's crucial to play to the organization's inherent strengths. After all, isn't this one of the pillars of strategic positioning, to determine the "competitive strengths"?

Large organizations possess extensive resources, established processes, and significant market influence. However, these advantages can also create inertia. To counteract this, large enterprises should leverage their resources to invest in innovative projects, while maintaining flexibility in their processes to adapt quickly to market changes.

In contrast, small businesses thrive on their agility and close-knit teams, which allow for swift decision-making and rapid adaptation. Their streamlined communication channels and direct access to leadership foster a culture of transparency and innovation. Small businesses should capitalize on these strengths by embracing iterative processes and continuous feedback loops, ensuring they remain responsive to customer needs and market trends.

By aligning transformation efforts with the organization's strengths, whether it's the resource abundance of large enterprises or the nimbleness of small businesses, companies can effectively navigate their ExO transformation journey and achieve sustainable growth.

Conclusion

Every organization needs to be able to perform, to have a here and now, while they also need to transform to have a future. As organizations embark on the journey to become Exponential Organizations (ExOs), it is crucial to approach the transformation with a clear understanding of the unique challenges and opportunities at hand. Implementing ExO attributes can drive significant innovation and growth, but it requires a significant effort to implement.

Before diving into the transformation process, organizations should conduct a thorough assessment of their current situation. This involves evaluating their existing capabilities, resources, and readiness for change. Engaging with an experienced coach or consultant can provide valuable insights and guidance during this assessment phase. Coaches bring expertise in navigating the complexities of ExO transformation, helping organizations identify potential roadblocks and devise effective strategies to overcome them. They can also run point on the change project and provide accountability.

One of the key steps in this assessment is to determine if the necessary prerequisites for transformation are present. This includes having strong leadership support, a culture open to innovation and experimentation, and established processes for driving continuous improvement. Organizations must ensure they have the foundational elements in place, such as a clearly defined Massive Transformative Purpose and aligned values, before attempting to implement other ExO attributes.

Moreover, organizations should be prepared to invest in the necessary tools and frameworks that facilitate the ExO transformation. The System & Soul (S2) framework, for example, integrates clarity and control with organizational culture and purpose, providing a structured approach that allows for embedding ExO principles. By mapping ExO attributes to its enabling S2 elements, businesses can create a structured pathway to achieve their transformation goals.

When facing problems or challenges during the transformation, organizations should revisit their initial analysis and adjust their strategies accordingly. Continuous feedback loops and iterative processes are essential to ensure that the transformation remains on track and adapts to emerging insights and changing conditions.

Embarking on an ExO transformation is a significant endeavor that requires careful planning, ongoing assessment, and robust support systems. By analyzing their situation, engaging experienced coaches, and ensuring foundational prerequisites, organizations of all sizes can successfully navigate their transformation journey and achieve exponential growth.

Contact

Huba Rostonics MSc, MBA

I help business leaders and teams get really clear on what's important in the next 90 days. GTM Strategist, Head of

Operations and Channel. System & Soul Business Coach. Best-Selling Author, EMMY nominated communicator.

https://www.linkedin.com/in/rostonics/

CHAPTER 9
GAME-CHANGING THE FUTURE OF BUSINESS

FABRIZIO GRAMUGLIO
And ExO Angels

Introduction > Defining Gamification

Gamification is the practice of applying game design elements and principles in non-game contexts to engage users and motivate desired behaviors[1]. It involves incorporating elements such as points, badges, leaderboards, challenges, and rewards into various applications, services, or processes to make them more enjoyable, engaging, and motivating[2].

The core idea behind gamification is to leverage people's natural inclination towards play and competition to encourage participation, learning, and productivity3. By introducing game-like mechanics, gamification aims to tap into intrinsic motivations, such as the desire for achievement, recognition, competition, and

---

[1] Deterding, S., Dixon, D., Khaled, R., & Nacke, L. (2011). From game design elements to gamefulness: defining "gamification". In Proceedings of the 15th international academic MindTrek conference: Envisioning future media environments (pp. 9-15).

[2] Zichermann, G., & Cunningham, C. (2011). Gamification by design: Implementing game mechanics in web and mobile apps. O'Reilly Media, Inc.

[3] Hamari, J., Koivisto, J., & Sarsa, H. (2014). Does gamification work?--a literature review of empirical studies on gamification. In 2014 47th Hawaii international conference on system sciences (pp. 3025-3034). IEEE.

self-expression, to foster engagement and drive desired outcomes[4].

Core Principles of Gamification

Gamification is built upon several core principles that contribute to its effectiveness[5]:

Motivation: Gamification leverages intrinsic and extrinsic motivations to engage users. Intrinsic motivations, such as enjoyment, personal growth, and a sense of accomplishment, are fostered through game-like experiences. Extrinsic motivations, like rewards, recognition, and competition, provide external incentives for participation.

Feedback and Progress: Clear and timely feedback mechanisms, such as points, levels, and progress bars, provide users with a sense of progress and achievement. These elements help users track their advancement and stay motivated throughout the experience.

Challenge and Mastery: Gamification incorporates challenges and skill-based progressions, allowing users to continuously improve and develop mastery. Well-designed challenges strike a balance between being achievable and providing a sense of accomplishment.

Social Interaction: Many gamification strategies incorporate social elements, such as leaderboards, team challenges, and social sharing, to foster competition, collaboration, and a sense of community among users.

---

[4] Nicholson, S. (2015). A recipe for meaningful gamification. In Gamification in education and business (pp. 1-20). Springer, Cham.

[5] Werbach, K., & Hunter, D. (2012). For the win: How game thinking can revolutionize your business. Wharton Digital Press.

Storytelling and Narrative: Gamification often employs narrative elements and storytelling techniques to create engaging and immersive experiences, providing context and meaning to the activities and challenges.

By leveraging these core principles, gamification aims to create engaging experiences that motivate users, foster desired behaviors, and ultimately achieve specific objectives, such as increased productivity, learning outcomes, customer engagement, or behavioral change[6].

Behavioral Impact of Gamification

Gamification leverages various psychological theories and principles to influence user behavior and drive desired outcomes. By understanding these underlying concepts, designers can create more effective and engaging gamified experiences. This section explores the psychological foundations of gamification, including motivation theories, reinforcement principles, and the role of intrinsic and extrinsic rewards.

Motivation Theories

Gamification draws heavily from established motivation theories to foster user engagement and sustained participation. Two prominent theories are:

Self-Determination Theory (SDT)[7]: This theory proposes that humans have three innate psychological needs: competence, autonomy, and relatedness. Gamification elements, such as

---

[6] Robson, K., Plangger, K., Kietzmann, J. H., McCarthy, I., & Pitt, L. (2015). Is it all a game? Understanding the principles of gamification. Business Horizons, 58(4), 411-420.

[7] Ryan, R. M., & Deci, E. L. (2000). Self-determination theory and the facilitation of intrinsic motivation, social development, and well-being. American psychologist, 55(1), 68.

challenges, choices, and social interactions, can fulfill these needs and promote intrinsic motivation.

Flow Theory[8]: Proposed by Mihaly Csikszentmihalyi, this theory describes the state of "flow," where individuals become fully immersed in an activity due to a balance between challenge and skill. Gamification aims to induce this state by providing appropriate levels of challenge and feedback.

Reinforcement Principles

Gamification employs reinforcement principles from operant conditioning, which suggests that behaviors can be shaped through the use of positive and negative reinforcements. Common reinforcement techniques used in gamification include:

Positive Reinforcement: Rewarding desired behaviors, such as earning points, badges, or virtual rewards, to increase the likelihood of those behaviors recurring.

Negative Reinforcement: Removing undesired stimuli or obstacles upon completing a desired behavior, such as unlocking new features or levels after achieving certain goals.

Schedules of Reinforcement: Varying the timing and frequency of reinforcements to maintain motivation and engagement, such as using variable ratio schedules for unpredictable rewards.

---

[8] M. Csikszentmihalyi (1990). Flow: The Psychology of Optimal Experience, Harper & Row

Intrinsic and Extrinsic Rewards

Gamification leverages both intrinsic and extrinsic rewards to motivate users[9]:

Intrinsic Rewards: These are internal, psychological rewards derived from the activity itself, such as a sense of accomplishment, personal growth, or enjoyment. Gamification elements like challenges, progress tracking, and narratives can tap into these intrinsic motivations.

Extrinsic Rewards: These are external rewards separate from the activity, such as points, badges, leaderboards, or tangible prizes. While effective in the short term, extrinsic rewards should be carefully balanced with intrinsic motivations to avoid undermining long-term engagement.

Gamification and Human Desires

Gamification's effectiveness lies in its ability to tap into fundamental human desires and motivations. By leveraging our innate drive for achievement, competition, and social recognition, gamification can influence user behaviors, foster engagement, and promote desired actions across various contexts.

Achievement and Mastery

Humans have an inherent desire for achievement and mastery, which stems from our need for competence and personal growth[10]. Gamification capitalizes on this desire by incorporating elements that provide a sense of progress, accomplishment, and

---

[9] Ryan, R. M., & Deci, E. L. (2000). Intrinsic and extrinsic motivations: Classic definitions and new directions. Contemporary educational psychology, 25(1), 54-67.

[10] Ryan, R. M., & Deci, E. L. (2000). Self-determination theory and the facilitation of intrinsic motivation, social development, and well-being. American psychologist, 55(1), 68.

skill development. Through features like levels, badges, progress bars, and skill-based challenges, gamification creates a sense of achievement and mastery, motivating users to continue engaging with the experience[11].

For example, in educational settings, gamification can introduce skill-based progressions and achievement levels, allowing students to track their progress and experience a sense of accomplishment as they advance through the material. This can foster a growth mindset and encourage continuous learning and skill development.

Competition and Social Recognition

Humans are inherently driven by the desire for competition and social recognition. Gamification taps into these desires by incorporating elements that enable users to compete with others, compare their performance, and receive recognition for their achievements[12].

Leaderboards, for instance, create a sense of competition by displaying users' ranks based on their performance or achievements. This social comparison and recognition can motivate users to strive for higher rankings and outperform their peers. Similarly, badges and achievements can serve as visible symbols of accomplishment, providing social recognition and status within the gamified environment.

In the workplace, gamification can leverage competitive elements like leaderboards and team challenges to foster friendly competition among employees, potentially increasing productivity

---

[11] Nicholson, S. (2015). A recipe for meaningful gamification. In Gamification in education and business (pp. 1-20). Springer, Cham

[12] Landers, R. N., Bauer, K. N., Callan, R. C., & Armstrong, M. B. (2015). Psychological theory and the gamification of learning. In Gamification in education and business (pp. 165-186). Springer, Cham

and performance as individuals or teams strive to outperform one another.

Influence on User Behaviors

By tapping into these fundamental human desires, gamification can effectively influence user behaviors and promote desired actions across various domains:

Engagement and Motivation: Gamification elements like challenges, rewards, and progress tracking can increase user engagement and motivation by providing a sense of achievement, competition, and continuous progress toward goals[13].

Habit Formation: Gamification can reinforce desired behaviors by consistently rewarding and reinforcing those actions, leading to the formation of habits over time[14].

Behavioral Change: Gamification can encourage users to adopt new behaviors or modify existing ones by presenting challenges, rewards, and social recognition for the desired actions[15].

Learning and Skill Development: By incorporating skill-based progressions, gamification can support learning and skill

---

[13] Sailer, M., Hense, J. U., Mayr, S. K., & Mandl, H. (2017). How gamification motivates: An experimental study of the effects of specific game design elements on psychological need satisfaction. Computers in Human Behavior, 69, 371-380.

[14] Eyal, N. (2014). Hooked: How to build habit-forming products. Penguin.

[15] Hamari, J., & Koivisto, J. (2015). Working out for likes: An empirical study on social influence in exercise gamification. Computers in Human Behavior, 50, 333-347.

development by providing a sense of accomplishment and mastery as users advance through increasingly challenging tasks[16].

Customer Engagement: In marketing and customer service contexts, gamification can foster customer engagement and loyalty by creating rewarding and enjoyable experiences that tap into users' desires for achievement, competition, and social recognition[17].

By understanding and leveraging these fundamental human desires, gamification designers can create engaging experiences that effectively influence user behaviors, promote desired actions, and ultimately achieve specific objectives across various domains.

Gamification Frameworks: our tool box

Gamification designers and practitioners have developed several frameworks to guide the design and implementation of gamified systems effectively. These frameworks provide structured approaches to understanding user motivations, identifying game elements, and aligning gamification strategies with desired outcomes. While there are numerous frameworks available, this section will highlight seven prominent ones, outlining their core principles and their relevance for businesses.

1. Octalysis Framework

Developed by Yu-kai Chou, the Octalysis Framework identifies eight core drives that motivate human behavior: epic meaning, development, and accomplishment, empowerment of creativity and feedback, ownership and possession, social influence and

---

[16] Kapp, K. M. (2012). *The gamification of learning and instruction: game-based methods and strategies for training and education*. John Wiley & Sons

[17] Robson, K., Plangger, K., Kietzmann, J. H., McCarthy, I., & Pitt, L. (2015). *Is it all a game? Understanding the principles of gamification*. Business Horizons, 58(4), 411-420.

relatedness, scarcity and impatience, unpredictability and curiosity, and loss and avoidance[18].

Wow Factor: The Octalysis Framework provides a comprehensive understanding of human motivations, enabling designers to craft gamified experiences that tap into multiple drives simultaneously.

Business Relevance: By aligning gamification elements with the appropriate motivational drives, businesses can enhance employee engagement, customer loyalty, and overall user experience.

2. Hexad User Types

Andrzej Marczewski's Hexad User Types framework categorizes users into six motivational types: achievers, socializers, free spirits, philanthropists, players, and disruptors[19]. This framework helps tailor gamification elements to different user preferences.

Wow Factor: The Hexad User Types framework recognizes the diversity of user motivations, enabling designers to create personalized and engaging experiences.

Business Relevance: By understanding their target audience's motivational types, businesses can develop tailored gamification strategies that resonate with their users, improving engagement and desired outcomes.

---

[18] Chou, Y. K. (2019). Actionable gamification: Beyond points, badges, and leaderboards. Packt Publishing Ltd.

[19] Marczewski, A. (2015). Even ninja monkeys like to play: Gamification, game thinking and motivational design. CreateSpace Independent Publishing Platform.

3. SAPS Framework

The SAPS Framework stands for Status, Access, Power, and Stuff. It categorizes game elements based on their ability to satisfy users' intrinsic motivations. This framework was developed by Gabe Zichermann[20].

Wow Factor: The SAPS Framework provides a structured approach to selecting and combining game elements that align with users' intrinsic motivations.

Business Relevance: By leveraging the SAPS Framework, businesses can create gamified experiences that tap into users' intrinsic motivations, fostering long-term engagement and behavior change.

4. Gamification Model Canvas

The Gamification Model Canvas, developed by Sergio Jiménez, is a visual tool that helps designers plan and document their gamification strategies[21]. It covers various aspects, including objectives, target behaviors, user types, game mechanics, and more.

Wow Factor: The Gamification Model Canvas offers a comprehensive and organized approach to designing gamified experiences, facilitating collaboration and communication among stakeholders.

Business Relevance: By utilizing the Gamification Model Canvas, businesses can streamline the design process, ensure

---

[20] Zichermann, G., & Cunningham, C. (2011). Gamification by Design: Implementing Game Mechanics in Web and Mobile Apps. O'Reilly Media, Inc.

[21] Design Thinking and Gamification: User Centered Methodologies Gamification Model Canvas by Sergio Jiménez

alignment with objectives, and increase the chances of successful gamification implementation.

5. Werbach's 6D Framework

Developed by Kevin Werbach and Dan Hunter, the 6D Framework consists of six steps: defining objectives, delineating target behaviors, describing players, devising activity loops, not forgetting the fun, and deploying appropriate tools[22].

Wow Factor: The 6D Framework provides a structured and iterative approach to gamification design, emphasizing the importance of aligning objectives, behaviors, and user motivations.

Business Relevance: By following the 6D Framework, businesses can ensure their gamification initiatives are well-designed, engaging, and effective in driving desired outcomes.

6. Gamification Gaia Framework

The Gamification Gaia Framework, developed by Gustavo Tondello, focuses on understanding user motivations and tailoring gamification elements accordingly[23]. It combines the Hexad User Types with the concept of "motivational affordances," which are game elements that satisfy specific motivations.

Wow Factor: The Gamification Gaia Framework offers a comprehensive approach to personalized gamification, ensuring that game elements align with individual user motivations.

---

[22] Werbach, K., & Hunter, D. (2012). For the win: How game thinking can revolutionize your business. Wharton Digital Press.

[23] Tondello, G. F., Valtchanov, D., Reetz, A., Wehbe, R. R., Orji, R., & Nacke, L. E. (2018). Towards a trait model of video game preferences. International Journal of Human-Computer Interaction, 34(8), 732-748.

Business Relevance: By implementing the Gamification Gaia Framework, businesses can create highly personalized and engaging experiences, leading to increased user satisfaction, retention, and desired behaviors.

7. Gamification Lens

The Gamification Lens, proposed by Brian Burke, provides a structured approach to evaluating and refining gamification designs[24]. It consists of five lenses: purpose, experience, feedback, dynamics, and context.

Wow Factor: The Gamification Lens offers a systematic way to analyze and improve gamification designs, ensuring they align with intended goals and provide an engaging user experience.

Business Relevance: By applying the Gamification Lens, businesses can evaluate and refine their gamification strategies, optimizing the user experience and increasing the likelihood of achieving desired outcomes.

These frameworks represent a subset of the numerous approaches available in the gamification field. While each framework has its unique strengths and focus areas, they all aim to provide structured guidance for designing effective and engaging gamified experiences. Businesses can leverage these frameworks to align their gamification initiatives with their objectives, target user motivations, and create compelling experiences that drive desired behaviors and outcomes. And talking about businesses, now it's time to bring everything back to business.

Section 3: Business Impact of Gamification

Gamification has the potential to deliver significant business benefits across various domains, including marketing, training,

---

[24] Burke, B. (2014). *Gamify: How gamification motivates people to do extraordinary things*. Routledge.

customer engagement, and employee productivity. By leveraging the motivational power of game elements and mechanics, businesses can enhance user experiences, drive desired behaviors, and achieve measurable outcomes[25].

This section explores the potential business impact of gamification, highlighting its applications, measurable outcomes, and key performance indicators (KPIs) for evaluating success[26].

Marketing and Customer Engagement

Gamification can be a powerful tool for marketing and customer engagement initiatives, helping businesses to attract and retain customers while fostering brand loyalty[27].

Applications:

Gamified loyalty programs and rewards systems
Interactive gamified advertising campaigns
Gamified product launches and promotions
Gamified customer support and feedback mechanisms
Measurable Outcomes and KPIs:
Customer acquisition and conversion rates
Customer retention and churn rates
Brand awareness and engagement metrics (e.g., social media interactions, website traffic)
Net Promoter Score (NPS) and customer satisfaction ratings

---

[25] Robson, K., Plangger, K., Kietzmann, J. H., McCarthy, I., & Pitt, L. (2015). Is it all a game? Understanding the principles of gamification. Business Horizons, 58(4), 411-420.

[26] Hamari, J., Koivisto, J., & Sarsa, H. (2014). Does gamification work?--a literature review of empirical studies on gamification. In 2014 47th Hawaii international conference on system sciences (pp. 3025-3034). IEEE

[27] Rodrigues, L. F., Oliveira, A., & Costa, C. J. (2016). Playing seriously–how gamification and social cues influence bank customers to use gamified e-business applications. Computers in Human Behavior, 63, 392-407.

Sales and revenue growth
Employee Training and Productivity
Gamification can be leveraged to enhance employee training programs, increase productivity, and foster a culture of continuous learning and improvement within organizations[28].

Applications:

Gamified onboarding and training programs[29]
Gamified performance management and goal-setting
Gamified ideation and innovation initiatives
Gamified workplace wellness and safety programs
Measurable Outcomes and KPIs:
Employee engagement and motivation levels
Training completion rates and knowledge retention
Productivity metrics (e.g., output, quality, efficiency)
Absenteeism and turnover rates
Cost savings and operational efficiency
Customer Support and Service
Gamification can be applied to customer support and service activities, improving customer experiences, fostering brand loyalty, and enhancing overall customer satisfaction.

Applications:

Gamified customer support portals and knowledge bases
Gamified troubleshooting and self-service tools
Gamified customer feedback and review mechanisms
Gamified customer communities and forums
Measurable Outcomes and KPIs:

---

[28] Sarangi, S., & Shah, S. (2015). Individuals, products and organizations: A gamification approach. In Gamification in Education and Business (pp. 269-297). Springer, Cham.

[29] Kapp, K. M. (2012). The gamification of learning and instruction: game-based methods and strategies for training and education. John Wiley & Sons.

Customer satisfaction scores (CSAT)
First-contact resolution rates
Customer effort scores (CES)
Customer retention and loyalty metrics
Cost savings from reduced support inquiries

Implementing Gamification Strategies

To effectively implement gamification strategies and measure their success, businesses should follow a structured approach[30]:

Define Clear Objectives: Establish specific, measurable, achievable, relevant, and time-bound (SMART) objectives aligned with business goals.

Identify Target Behaviors: Determine the desired behaviors or actions you want to encourage or reinforce through gamification.

Understand User Motivations: Leverage user research and frameworks (e.g., Octalysis, Hexad User Types) to understand your target audience's motivations and preferences.

Design Gamified Experiences: Develop engaging gamified experiences by incorporating appropriate game elements and mechanics that align with user motivations and desired behaviors.

Establish Metrics and KPIs: Define specific metrics and KPIs that will be used to measure the success of your gamification initiatives, aligned with your objectives.

Monitor and Iterate: Continuously monitor the performance of your gamified experiences, gather user feedback, and iterate based on data-driven insights to optimize engagement and outcomes.

By following this structured approach and tracking relevant metrics and KPIs, businesses can effectively evaluate the impact

---

[30] Xu, Y. (2011). Literature review on web application gamification and analytics. CSDL Technical Report 11-05, Department of Computer Science, University of Hawaii at Manoa.

of their gamification strategies and make informed decisions to refine and optimize their initiatives for maximum business impact.

To illustrate the practical applications and potential impact of gamification, this chapter presents real-world case studies of businesses that have successfully implemented gamification strategies across various industries and objectives. These examples showcase how companies have leveraged game elements and mechanics to drive user acquisition, customer retention, employee training, and other desired outcomes, quantifying the results and return on investment (ROI) whenever possible.

Gamification Case Studies

Case Study 1: Samsung Nation (Marketing and Customer Engagement)

Samsung Nation is a gamified online community and loyalty program created by Samsung to engage with its customers and promote brand loyalty. The platform incorporates various gamification elements, including badges, leaderboards, and challenges, rewarding users for activities such as participating in forums, contributing content, and referring friends.

Objectives:

Increase customer engagement and brand loyalty
Foster a vibrant online community of Samsung enthusiasts
Promote product education and peer-to-peer support

Results:

Over 1.3 million registered users as of 2021[31]

---

[31] Samsung Nation. (2021). About Samsung Nation. Retrieved from https://www.samsung.com/us/samsung-nation/

Increased customer advocacy and brand loyalty, with active community members being 67% more likely to recommend Samsung products

Estimated cost savings of $5 million per year by leveraging the community for product education and support[32]

Case Study 2: Deloitte Leadership Academy (Employee Training)

Deloitte, a leading professional services firm, implemented a gamified leadership development program called the "Leadership Academy" to engage and train its employees. The program incorporates game elements such as missions, badges, leaderboards, and progress tracking to motivate employees and facilitate learning.

Objectives:

Enhance leadership skills and competencies among employees
Increase engagement and completion rates for leadership training
Foster a culture of continuous learning and development

Results:

Over 50,000 employees participated in the program[33]

---

[32] Hoffman, R. (2020). Samsung Nation: A Customer Engagement Game Changer. Retrieved from https://www.bunchball.com/blog/post/1359/samsung-nation-a-customer-engagement-game-changer

[33] Deloitte. (2020). Deloitte Leadership Academy. Retrieved from https://www2.deloitte.com/us/en/pages/about-deloitte/articles/leadership-academy.html Robson, K., Plangger, K., Kietzmann, J. H., McCarthy, I., & Pitt, L. (2020). Game on: Engaging customers and employees through gamification. Business Horizons, 63(5)

37% increase in leadership course completion rates compared to traditional training methods

Improved leadership capabilities and career advancement opportunities for participants[34]

Case Study 3: Strava (Fitness and Wellness)

Strava is a popular fitness tracking and social networking app that leverages gamification to motivate users and foster a sense of community. The app incorporates elements such as challenges, leaderboards, badges, and social sharing to encourage users to track and share their fitness activities.

Objectives:

Motivate users to engage in regular physical activity and fitness
Foster a community of fitness enthusiasts and social support
Increase user engagement and retention

Results:

Over 100 million registered users as of 2022[35]

Users who participate in challenges are 2.5 times more likely to remain active on the platform[36]

---

[34] Deloitte. (2021). Deloitte Leadership Academy: Empowering Leaders for What's Next. Retrieved from https://www2.deloitte.com/content/dam/Deloitte/us/Documents/about-deloitte/us-deloitte-leadership-academy-brochure.pdf

[35] Strava. (2022). About Strava. Retrieved from https://www.strava.com/about

[36] Strava. (2020). Strava Challenges: Motivating Millions to Move More. Retrieved from https://blog.strava.com/press/strava-challenges-motivating-millions-to-move-more/

Increased user engagement and retention, with users logging over 8 billion activities on the platform[37]

These case studies demonstrate the versatility of gamification and its potential to drive desired outcomes across various business domains, from marketing and customer engagement to employee training and fitness/wellness. By leveraging game elements and mechanics aligned with specific objectives, businesses can create engaging experiences that motivate users, foster communities, and ultimately achieve measurable results and ROI.

Do you want to know more? Don't miss the "Comprehensive List of 90+ Gamification Examples & Cases with ROI Stats (2024)"[38]

ROI and Measurement of Gamification Initiatives

Implementing gamification strategies requires a significant investment of resources, including development costs, implementation expenses, and ongoing maintenance efforts. As such, businesses must measure the return on investment (ROI) of their gamification initiatives to justify the allocation of resources and demonstrate the tangible business value generated. This chapter discusses the importance of measuring ROI, provides a framework for calculating it, and highlights key performance indicators (KPIs) and metrics that businesses should track to evaluate the effectiveness of their gamification efforts.

Importance of Measuring ROI

Measuring the ROI of gamification initiatives is essential for several reasons:

---

[37] Strava. (2022). Strava Metro: Understanding Human Movement. Retrieved from https://metro.strava.com/

[38] https://yukaichou.com/gamification-examples/gamification-stats-figures/

Justifying Investment: By quantifying the financial returns, businesses can justify the initial and ongoing investments in gamification strategies to stakeholders and decision-makers[39].

Demonstrating Business Value: ROI calculations provide concrete evidence of the business value generated by gamification, beyond just user engagement and participation metrics[40].

Continuous Improvement: Measuring ROI enables businesses to identify areas for optimization, refine their gamification strategies, and maximize returns over time[41].

Benchmarking and Comparison: ROI metrics allow businesses to compare the performance of different gamification initiatives, helping them prioritize and allocate resources effectively.

Calculating ROI for Gamification Initiatives

To calculate the ROI of a gamification initiative, businesses should follow a structured framework that considers both the costs and measurable business outcomes. Here's a general approach:

Identify Direct Costs: Calculate the direct costs associated with the gamification initiative, including development costs,

---

[39] Robson, K., Plangger, K., Kietzmann, J. H., McCarthy, I., & Pitt, L. (2020). Is it all a game? Understanding the principles of gamification. Business Horizons, 63(3), 391-402.

[40] Rodrigues, L. F., Oliveira, A., & Costa, C. J. (2021). Playing seriously–how gamification and social cues influence bank customers to use gamified e-business applications. Computers in Human Behavior, 120, 106726.

[41] Hamari, J., & Koivisto, J. (2020). Working out for likes: An empirical study on social influence in exercise gamification. Computers in Human Behavior, 102, 336-347.

implementation expenses, technology infrastructure, and ongoing maintenance[42].

Estimate Indirect Costs: Consider any indirect costs, such as employee training, marketing expenses, or opportunity costs related to the initiative[43].

Define Measurable Business Outcomes: Identify the specific business outcomes you aim to achieve through gamification, such as increased sales, improved customer retention, higher employee productivity, or reduced training costs[44].

Quantify the Benefits: Assign monetary values to the measurable business outcomes achieved through gamification, based on industry benchmarks, historical data, or conservative estimates[45].

Calculate ROI: Use the following formula to calculate the ROI: ROI = (Total Benefits - Total Costs) / Total Costs × 100%[46]

By following this framework and accurately quantifying the costs and benefits, businesses can calculate the ROI of their

---

[42] Kapp, K. M. (2021). The gamification of learning and instruction: game-based methods and strategies for training and education. John Wiley & Sons.

[43] Sarangi, S., & Shah, S. (2021). Individuals, products and organizations: A gamification approach. In Gamification in Education and Business (pp. 269-297). Springer, Cham.

[44] Rodrigues, L. F., Oliveira, A., & Costa, C. J. (2020). Playing seriously—how gamification and social cues influence bank customers to use gamified e-business applications. Computers in Human Behavior, 103, 245-256.

[45] Robson, K., Plangger, K., Kietzmann, J. H., McCarthy, I., & Pitt, L. (2021). Game on: Engaging customers and employees through gamification. Business Horizons, 64(4), 459-471.

[46] Xu, Y. (2012). Literature review on web application gamification and analytics. (CSDL Technical Report 11–05). University of Hawaii,

gamification initiatives, enabling informed decision-making and resource allocation.

Additionally, by consistently tracking and analyzing KPIs and metrics (see previous sections), businesses can gain a comprehensive understanding of the effectiveness of their gamification initiatives, enabling data-driven decision-making and continuous optimization for maximum ROI.

Best Practices, Considerations, and Ethics in Gamification

Implementing gamification successfully requires careful planning, design, and execution. This chapter shares best practices and tips for designing and implementing effective gamification strategies while also addressing potential pitfalls, challenges, and ethical considerations that businesses should be aware of.

Best Practices for Effective Gamification

Align with Business Objectives: Ensure that gamification strategies are aligned with clear business objectives and desired outcomes, such as increased engagement, productivity, or customer loyalty[47].

Understand User Motivations: Conduct user research and leverage frameworks like the Octalysis Model or Hexad User Types to understand user motivations and tailor gamification elements accordingly[48].

Balance Extrinsic and Intrinsic Rewards: Combine extrinsic rewards (e.g., points, badges) with intrinsic rewards (e.g., sense of

---

[47] Robson, K., Plangger, K., Kietzmann, J. H., McCarthy, I., & Pitt, L. (2022). Game on: Engaging customers and employees through gamification. Business Horizons, 65(3), 367-381.

[48] Tondello, G. F., Valtchanov, D., Reetz, A., Wehbe, R. R., Orji, R., & Nacke, L. E. (2021). Towards a trait model of video game preferences. International Journal of Human-Computer Interaction, 37(8), 713-728.

accomplishment, autonomy) to foster sustained engagement and avoid over-reliance on external motivators[49].

Provide Clear Goals and Feedback: Set clear goals and provide timely feedback mechanisms, such as progress bars and leaderboards, to help users track their progress and achievements[50].

Foster Social Interactions: Incorporate social elements like team challenges, social sharing, and community features to foster collaboration, competition, and a sense of belonging[51].

Iterate and Optimize: Continuously monitor user engagement, gather feedback, and analyze data to refine and optimize gamification strategies for better results[52].

Potential Pitfalls and Challenges

Overemphasis on Extrinsic Rewards: An overreliance on extrinsic rewards can undermine intrinsic motivation and lead to disengagement once the rewards are removed[53].

---

[49] Rodrigues, L. F., Oliveira, A., & Costa, C. J. (2021). Playing seriously–how gamification and social cues influence bank customers to use gamified e-business applications. Computers in Human Behavior, 120, 106726.

[50] Kapp, K. M. (2021). The gamification of learning and instruction: game-based methods and strategies for training and education. John Wiley & Sons.

[51] Hamari, J., & Koivisto, J. (2020). Working out for likes: An empirical study on social influence in exercise gamification. Computers in Human Behavior, 102, 336-347.

[52] Xu, Y. (2022). Gamification and Analytics: A Comprehensive Guide to Measuring Success. CRC Press.

[53] Rodrigues, L. F., Oliveira, A., & Costa, C. J. (2020). Playing seriously–how gamification and social cues influence bank customers to use gamified e-business applications. Computers in Human Behavior, 103, 245-256.

Poorly Designed Mechanics: Poorly designed game mechanics or imbalanced challenges can lead to frustration, disengagement, or undesirable behaviors[54].

User Fatigue and Saturation: Users may experience fatigue or saturation if gamification elements become repetitive or fail to evolve over time[55].

Data Privacy and Security Concerns: Gamification initiatives may involve collecting and storing user data, raising privacy and security concerns that need to be addressed.

Resistance and Skepticism: Some users or stakeholders may be skeptical or resistant to gamification, perceiving it as gimmicky or inappropriate for certain contexts[56].

Ethical Considerations

Transparency and Consent: Clearly communicate the purpose and mechanics of gamification initiatives, and obtain user consent for data collection and usage.

Avoid Manipulation and Coercion: Gamification should not coerce or manipulate users into undesirable behaviors or actions that go against their interests or values.

Inclusive and Fair Design: Ensure that gamification strategies are inclusive and fair, avoiding biases or discrimination based on factors like gender, age, or ability.

---

[54] Kapp, K. M. (2022). The gamification of learning and instruction: game-based methods and strategies for training and education (2nd ed.). Pfeiffer.

[55] Sarangi, S., & Shah, S. (2022). Gamification in Organizations: Enhancing Engagement and Performance. Routledge.

[56] Robson, K., Plangger, K., Kietzmann, J. H., McCarthy, I., & Pitt, L. (2020). Is it all a game? Understanding the principles of gamification. Business Horizons, 63(3), 391-402.

Privacy and Data Protection: Implement robust data privacy and security measures to protect user data and comply with relevant regulations.

Responsible Use of Persuasive Techniques: Exercise caution and ethical judgment when using persuasive techniques, such as social proofing or scarcity, to influence user behavior.

By following best practices, addressing potential pitfalls, and adhering to ethical guidelines, businesses can increase the chances of successful gamification implementation while fostering trust, engagement, and positive outcomes for all stakeholders.

Gamification for Community Impact <insert case studies>

Gamification has the potential to foster community engagement, collaboration, and participation in various contexts beyond traditional business settings. This chapter explores how gamification can be leveraged to enhance community-related activities, such as education, healthcare, and civic engagement, while also analyzing the potential benefits and drawbacks of this approach.

Fostering Community Engagement and Collaboration

Gamification can be an effective tool for encouraging community engagement and collaboration by tapping into intrinsic motivations and creating a sense of shared purpose and achievement. By incorporating game elements such as challenges, leaderboards, and social sharing features, gamification can foster a spirit of friendly competition and camaraderie among community members.

For example, in neighborhood or community-based initiatives, gamification can be used to incentivize and track participation in activities such as recycling programs, community clean-ups, or volunteering efforts. By awarding points, badges, or other rewards for completing tasks or reaching milestones, gamification can motivate individuals to contribute to the collective effort while fostering a sense of community pride and accomplishment.

Examples of Gamification in Community Contexts

Education: Gamification has been widely adopted in educational settings to enhance student engagement, motivation, and learning outcomes. Platforms like Classcraft and Kahoot! incorporate game elements like avatars, experience points, and quests to make learning more interactive and enjoyable[57]. Additionally, gamification can foster collaboration among students through group challenges and team-based activities.

Healthcare: In the healthcare sector, gamification has been used to promote healthy behaviors, improve patient adherence to treatment plans, and encourage community participation in wellness initiatives. For example, apps like Zombies, Run! and StepBet gamify physical activity by incorporating narratives, challenges, and social elements[58]. Similarly, gamified health education programs can increase community awareness and engagement around important health topics.

Civic Engagement: Gamification can be applied to encourage civic engagement and participation in community-related decision-making processes. Platforms like Civic Champs and Civiq employ game mechanics like points, badges, and leaderboards to incentivize community members to participate in

---

[57] Majuri, J., Koivisto, J., & Hamari, J. (2018). Gamification of education and learning: A review of empirical literature. In Proceedings of the 2nd International GamiFIN Conference (pp. 11-19).

[58] Sardi, L., Idri, A., & Fernández-Alemán, J. L. (2017). A systematic review of gamification in e-Health. Journal of biomedical informatics, 71, 31-48.

local events, provide feedback on civic issues, or contribute to crowdsourced projects[59].

Potential Benefits and Drawbacks

Gamification in community contexts can offer numerous potential benefits, including:

Increased engagement and participation in community-related activities: By leveraging game elements like challenges, rewards, and social interactions, gamification can tap into intrinsic motivations and make community activities more enjoyable and compelling, leading to higher levels of involvement and sustained participation[60].

Enhanced collaboration and social cohesion among community members: Gamification strategies that incorporate team-based challenges, leaderboards, and social sharing features can foster a sense of camaraderie and community spirit, encouraging collaboration and strengthening social bonds[61].

Improved learning outcomes and knowledge retention in educational settings: Gamified learning environments can make educational content more interactive, engaging, and memorable,

---

[59] L. Hassan, J. Hamari (2020). Gamification in civic engagement: A study on motivations for participation. In 2016 International Conference on Collaboration Technologies and Systems.

[60] Koivisto, J., & Hamari, J. (2019). The rise of motivational information systems: A review of gamification research. International Journal of Information Management, 45, 191-210.

[61] Rodrigues, L. F., Oliveira, A., & Costa, C. J. (2021). Playing seriously--how gamification and social cues influence bank customers to use gamified e-business applications. Computers in Human Behavior, 120, 106726.

leading to better knowledge acquisition and retention among students[62].

Promotion of healthy behaviors and lifestyle changes in healthcare contexts: By gamifying fitness activities, treatment adherence, and health education programs, gamification can motivate individuals to adopt and sustain positive health behaviors within their communities[63].

Greater transparency and inclusivity in civic decision-making processes: Gamified civic engagement platforms can encourage more diverse and widespread community participation in local decision-making processes, fostering transparency and ensuring that a variety of perspectives and voices are heard.

Fostering a sense of purpose and accomplishment: By setting clear goals, providing feedback, and recognizing achievements, gamification can instill a sense of purpose and accomplishment among community members, reinforcing their commitment to collective efforts[64].

However, it is essential to consider potential drawbacks and challenges, such as:

- Concerns over the commodification of community-related activities or values
- Potential for gamification to become a superficial or short-term motivator

---

[62] Kapp, K. M. (2021). The gamification of learning and instruction: game-based methods and strategies for training and education. John Wiley & Sons.

[63] Hamari, J., & Koivisto, J. (2020). Working out for likes: An empirical study on social influence in exercise gamification. Computers in Human Behavior, 102, 336-347.

[64] Xu, Y. (2022). Gamification and Analytics: A Comprehensive Guide to Measuring Success. CRC Press.

- Ethical considerations regarding data privacy and the responsible use of persuasive techniques
- Ensuring inclusivity and accessibility for all community members, regardless of age, ability, or technological proficiency

To mitigate these challenges, it is crucial to design gamification strategies that align with the community's core values, prioritize intrinsic motivations, and involve community members in the design and implementation process. Additionally, adhering to ethical guidelines and data privacy best practices is essential for building trust and ensuring the responsible use of gamification in community contexts.

Conclusion

Throughout this chapter, we have explored the powerful concept of gamification and its potential to transform various aspects of our lives, from businesses to communities. By leveraging game design elements and mechanics in non-game contexts, gamification taps into our innate human desires for achievement, competition, and social recognition, fostering engagement and driving desired behaviors.

Key Takeaways:

Understanding Gamification: We defined gamification as the practice of applying game design principles to non-game contexts, aiming to enhance user engagement, motivation, and desired outcomes. We delved into the core principles of gamification, such as leveraging intrinsic and extrinsic motivations, providing clear feedback and progress tracking, incorporating challenges and social interactions, and employing storytelling techniques. Psychological Foundations: Gamification draws from established psychological theories, including Self-Determination Theory, Flow Theory, and principles of operant conditioning. By aligning with these theories, gamification strategies can effectively tap into users' intrinsic motivations, induce a state of flow, and reinforce desired behaviors through positive and negative reinforcements.

Influencing Human Behavior: Gamification capitalizes on fundamental human desires for achievement, competition, and social recognition. By incorporating elements like levels, badges, leaderboards, and social sharing features, gamification can influence user behaviors, foster engagement, promote habit formation, facilitate learning, and drive customer loyalty.

Gamification Frameworks: We explored various frameworks designed to guide the effective implementation of gamification, such as the Octalysis Framework, Hexad User Types, SAPS Framework, Gamification Model Canvas, Werbach's 6D Framework, Gamification Gaia Framework, and Gamification Lens. These frameworks provide structured approaches to understanding user motivations, identifying game elements, and aligning gamification strategies with desired outcomes.

Business Impact: Gamification offers substantial benefits across various business domains, including marketing, customer engagement, employee training, and productivity. By leveraging gamification, businesses can increase customer acquisition and retention, foster brand loyalty, enhance employee engagement and performance, and achieve measurable outcomes and return on investment (ROI).

Case Studies: Real-world examples, such as Samsung Nation, Deloitte Leadership Academy, and Strava, demonstrated the successful implementation of gamification strategies, quantifying results like increased user engagement, improved training completion rates, and sustained activity levels.

ROI and Measurement: We discussed the importance of measuring the ROI of gamification initiatives, providing a framework for calculating costs, benefits, and tangible business outcomes. Additionally, we highlighted key performance indicators (KPIs) and metrics that businesses should track to evaluate the effectiveness of their gamification efforts.

Best Practices and Considerations: We shared best practices for designing and implementing effective gamification strategies, including aligning with business objectives, understanding user motivations, balancing extrinsic and intrinsic rewards, providing clear goals and feedback, fostering social interactions, and continuously iterating based on data-driven insights. We also addressed potential pitfalls, challenges, and ethical considerations surrounding gamification implementation.

Community Impact: Gamification can foster community engagement, collaboration, and participation in various contexts, such as education, healthcare, and civic engagement. By leveraging game elements and social interactions, gamification can promote learning, encourage healthy behaviors, and facilitate inclusive decision-making processes within communities.

The Future of Gamification:

As we look ahead, the potential applications and impact of gamification continue to expand. With advances in technology, data analytics, and user experience design, we can expect gamification strategies to become increasingly personalized, adaptive, and seamlessly integrated into our daily lives.

In the business realm, gamification will play a pivotal role in enhancing employee engagement, driving customer loyalty, and optimizing operational processes. Companies that embrace gamification principles will have a competitive edge in attracting and retaining top talent, fostering a culture of continuous learning and innovation, and delivering exceptional customer experiences.

Moreover, gamification will continue to shape the way we approach community-building, education, and social impact initiatives. Gamified platforms and applications will empower individuals to actively participate in their communities, acquire knowledge in engaging ways, and contribute to solving societal challenges through collective efforts and friendly competition.

As the boundaries between the physical and digital worlds blur, gamification will permeate various aspects of our lives, making everyday tasks and experiences more enjoyable, motivating, and rewarding. By harnessing the power of game design principles, we can unlock new levels of engagement, productivity, and personal growth.

However, it is crucial to remember that gamification is not a panacea; its success relies on thoughtful implementation, ethical considerations, and a deep understanding of user motivations and behaviors. Responsible gamification practices that prioritize intrinsic motivations, transparency, and inclusivity will be key to ensuring positive outcomes and fostering trust among users.

Contact Us:

We invite you to explore the exciting world of gamification further and stay updated on the latest trends, best practices, and success stories. Connect with us on our website https://exoangels.com or follow us on Linkedin to join a community of gamification enthusiasts, experts, and practitioners.

Together, we can harness the power of gamification to create engaging experiences, drive positive change, and unlock the full potential of human motivation and achievement.

**The Future of Business
Applied gamification**

As rapid technological progress accelerates industry disruption, businesses must evolve to stay competitive and relevant. Emerging innovations like artificial intelligence, decentralized finance, and blockchain present both immense opportunities and existential threats across sectors. For companies to successfully navigate this tumultuous landscape, they need more than just new products and systems - they require fundamental mindset shifts.

This reality drives the imperative for progressive leadership development centered around forward-thinking methodologies that empower organizations to embrace change. Pioneering firms are turning to gamification principles as a catalyst for this critical cultural transformation.

Rather than simplistic "gamification" veneers of points and badges, modern gamification applies comprehensive insights from game theory (the mathematical study of strategic decision-making), motivational psychology, and serious gaming (games designed for non-entertainment purposes like training and education). By systematically embedding these intrinsic motivational drivers into operations, companies prime their people for the futures they wish to create rather than desperately clinging to fading conventions.

Emerging DeFi and Blockchain Upstarts

Nowhere is this gamification mindset more evident than in the rapidly evolving realm of decentralized finance and blockchain-enabled business models. As cryptocurrencies, NFTs, DAOs, and Web3 disrupt global financial services, pioneering blockchain startups are leveraging motivational design principles from the outset to cultivate loyal, invested communities of users and contributors.

A prime example is the popular Defi protocol Aave and its gamified governance model that taps into psychological drives around ownership, accomplishment, and status. By staking their crypto tokens, community members accumulate voting power as well as expanding rewards and lending opportunities enabled by the Aave platform itself. People remain actively involved not just for profits, but because they feel a sense of meaningful progression tied to the protocol's growth.

Similarly, gaming platform Skyweaver melds NFT collecting with a play-to-earn model that monetizes desired experiences around unpredictability and surprise. As players battle and accumulate randomized "loot boxes" containing unique NFT cards and in-game assets, they get dopamine hits from the variability and mystery of potential rewards. This variability of reinforcement maintains Skyweaver's addictive appeal and user retention in a saturated market.

Projects like Dohrnii showcase the power of combining multiple motivational drivers through its social DeFi stack. While offering standard financial primitives like lending, borrowing, and staking, the protocol layers on tools for collective investing, community reputation scores, and achievement badging. People derive ongoing satisfaction not just from financial upside, but from the social influence, sense of ownership, and goal-driven progression their involvement confers.

Beyond gamifying individual products, smart blockchain founders recognize the imperative of stoking intrinsic motivations like epic meaning (the core drive of grand, inspiring missions tied to vast positive impact) for long-term sustainability and traction. Ethereum itself originated as a revolutionary movement to realize Vitalik Buterin's world-changing vision for decentralized coordination technology that democratizes opportunity. Embodying this heroic purpose establishes resilient cultures of passionate contributors rather than mercurial speculators merely chasing hype cycles.

From fundraising, all the way through perpetual operations, companies integrating even basic principles of motivational design are gaining powerful community advantages as they reinvent industries like finance through DeFi and the distributed web. More importantly, they demonstrate how proactively embedding human psychology into foundational architectures maximizes an organization's resilience and agility required to thrive amid future unknowns.

AI and Automation's Human Stakes

The looming disruption from artificial intelligence and large-scale automation across major industries also mandates a fundamental rethinking of how companies design roles, compensation, training, and cultural narratives to optimally integrate with human motivations. Simply replicating current industrial norms and processes derived from legacy command-and-control management philosophies will likely yield dehumanizing, dystopian consequences on a massive scale.

Unfortunately, today's change-resistant corporate cultures often prioritize narrow productivity metrics over nurturing intrinsic drivers of human flourishing like creativity, growth, social connections, and transcendent meaning. In this environment, gamification empowers enlightened leaders to spearhead grassroots cultural renovation from the inside out.

Pioneering AI firms on the vanguard like Anthropic are cultivating loyal, mission-driven cultures by appealing to core motivations like epic meaning/calling and loss avoidance. They've articulated an inspirational "Massive Transformative Purpose" to develop artificial general intelligence for the benefit of humanity while responsibly mitigating existential risks that could lead to irreversible negative outcomes. The gravity of this world-spanning mission instills employees with a sense of heroic, generational importance rarely found in the tech world.

Furthermore, Anthropic transparently details robust AI safety practices and ethical constraints like debate training and constitutional rulebooks in its system development. This radical openness around proactively confronting potential hazards instills faith that their hardworking teams aren't recklessly sprinting towards a dystopic, Terminator-esque fate. Employees can feel confident their diligent efforts and accomplishments will durably matter rather than being rendered obsolete or destructive by shortsighted pursuits.

Other pioneering AI labs recognize the existential imperative of embedding gameplay motivations right into the core design and personality of their algorithms and user experiences. This proactively safeguards against dehumanizing AI-human interactions that could corrode vital wellsprings of human inventiveness and sense-making over time.

For instance, Anthropic has infused its breakthrough AI language models like Claude with friendly, empathetic personas that communicate with emotional intelligence and social awareness. Instead of sterile, robotic pattern-matching, these systems uphold contextualized conversation flow building real interpersonal connections. This designed sociability builds abiding trust while stoking people's curiosity, autonomous sense-making desires, and feelings of bonded kinship in a manner cold, antiseptic data processing cannot.

By baking in thoughtful motivational design centered on lasting human cravings for discovery, growth, and belongingness from the ground up, innovators ensure transformative AI systems form a nourishing symbiosis with our species rather than adversarial, alienating relationships. Humanizing AI through motivational psychology creates collaborative partnerships intuitively optimized for the unique strengths and abilities of each side from day one.

Manufacturing and Industrial Giants

While blockchain and artificial intelligence understandably dominate future industry narratives around disruption and progress, the paradigm-shifting innovations poised to upend traditional sectors like manufacturing, logistics, and heavy industrials are no less momentous. As cutting-edge technologies like additive manufacturing, industrial internet of things (IoT) predictive analytics, cloud automation, and smart sensor integration proliferate throughout global supply chains, the battle to attract and maintain motivated human capital becomes even more paramount.

Industry stalwarts like GE, Rolls Royce, Bosch, and their small-to-midsized counterparts are moving aggressively to rearchitect entrenched ecosystems around new models of worker experience and motivation. From the factory floor to the C-suite, these behemoths recognize embedding gamification and motivational architecture into workflows, compensation systems, training frameworks, and cultural rituals represents an existential operational imperative.

For example, innovators are revamping intra-logistics and smart warehousing facilities by infusing motivational forces like unpredictability, accomplishment, and social influence into automated picking, packing, and sortation workflows. Rather than devolving into soulless human monitoring of autonomous systems, thoughtful gamification unlocks engaged flow states of thrilling operational mastery.

Warehouse technologies imbued with gameplay drivers like dynamically replenishing surprise challenge modes, quantified skill progression paths, and collaborative team competitions unlock deep wells of human potential. What could have devolved into dystopian drudgery instead unleashes the boundless capabilities of people seamlessly interfacing with technology in symbiotic experience superhighways.

Crucially, this integration moves far beyond trite "gamification" gimmicks like simplistic points, badges, and leaderboards slapped atop stagnant industrial processes. The motivational architecture blueprints enabled by modern gamification frameworks allow innovators to fundamentally reconceive every process, incentive system, and workflow around the first principles of innate human desire. Physical work itself becomes intrinsically invigorating because it's reverse-engineered from the ground up to activate our species' evolutionary cravings for discovery, growth, and social signaling.

By strategically aligning sociotechnical systems with core motivational drives, forward-thinking manufacturers unlock a uniquely human-centered path to progress. Technology no longer dictates the terms of human experience - expansive ambition and actualized potential beckon technology to its highest expression in symbiotic service.

SMBs Transforming Through Motivation

While case studies often highlight the bleeding-edge pursuits of tech titans, billion-dollar venture darlings, and globe-spanning industrial conglomerates, the reality is organizations of all sizes and industries are strategically adopting gamification to fortify their cultures and competitive advantages.

Small-to-midsized businesses (SMBs) represent over 90% of the business population comprising the backbone of local job creation and economic growth worldwide. For these vital enterprises striving to attract top talent and foster progressive cultures, incorporating gameplay motivations signals a forward-leaning, human-first ethos.

A local professional services firm might redesign employee onboarding around escalating challenge streams that immerse new hires in the company's skills and values through self-directed mastery progression. A regional manufacturer could install interactive digital terminals across the warehouse that randomize team-based sortation competitions to inspire friendly rivalry and sustained operations engagement.

Meanwhile, a healthcare system may issue verified, blockchain-credentialed badges to patients for accomplishing preventative health regimens, combining motivations of ownership, achievement, and trust. Even a small town's main street businesses stand to boost marketing effectiveness by launching collaborative progress-chasing puzzles unlocking exclusive local offers and rewards.

The key commonality across these diverse use cases is centering the modernized employee and customer experiences on cultivating intrinsic desire through smartly embedded gameplay motivators. Businesses masterfully tapping into the core drivers of modern motivation will magnetically attract the best human resources in their markets.

Blending Hearts and Minds for Impact

Across industries as diverse as finance, AI, manufacturing, and local services, one unifying truth materializes - the most future-resilient organizations proactively cultivate passionate, motivated cultures as strategic necessities. Simply adopting the latest technologies offers no sustainable protection against disruption. Motivational strategies that intrinsically inspire change-embracing mindsets forge true adaptability.

Whether gamifying protocol participation, humanizing machine interactions, infusing smart operations with invigorating ambition, or embedding mastery streams into everyday services, principled applications of motivational psychology realize this human imperative. While the technical specifics vary, architectures centered on our deeply rooted cravings for progress, belonging, trust, and meaning create the foundations for relentless invention and impact delivery.

Through advanced integration of core motivators like epic meaning, accomplishment, unpredictability, and social influence, pioneering leaders transcend building engaging products. They purposefully cultivate organizations where people relentlessly pursue growth because their aspirations have become institutionalized drivers.

This fusion of impassioned motivation with innovative capability represents the supreme competitive advantage in our exponentially changing world. While technologies will always march forward, instilling indelible human ambition and desire within your organization establishes the psychological foundations for resilient reinvention no matter the disruption.

The visionaries who masterfully wield these motivational tools won't just survive upheaval - they'll joyfully create the realities that bestow epic meaning upon us all. Humanity's most inspiring future innovations flow not from rote execution, but the boundless potential of wholehearted Being actualizing itself into dynamic Becoming.

If you're inspired to elevate your enterprise to these heroic heights of impact, inquire today about our comprehensive leadership immersions exploring motivational transformation. We'll equip your team with powerful frameworks for systematically embedding game psychology that turns your people's intrinsic desires into sustained world-changing results.

Those prepared to gamify the human experience itself will inherit the future. The opportunity awaits you and your organization to become the motivators who reshape reality through passionate, motivated co-creation. Will you step forward to play your role?

Contact us to identify trends, best practices, and success stories. Connect with us on our website https://exoangels.com or follow us on Linkedin to join a community of gamification enthusiasts, experts, and practitioners.

Fabrizio Gramulglio

Futurist & Exponential Advisor | Passionate Innovator | Technology Enthusiast | Mentor & Speaker on Exponential Growth & Disruption

https://www.linkedin.com/in/gramuglio/

CHAPTER 10
DEMOCRATIZING FINANCE:
LEVERAGING DEFI IN AN ORGANIZATION

Rob Bassani

Decentralized Finance (DeFi) has emerged as one of the most transformative innovations within the blockchain and cryptocurrency space. By leveraging blockchain technology, DeFi aims to decentralize and democratize traditional financial systems, enabling open, permissionless, and borderless access to financial services. This chapter explores the major themes of DeFi, with a particular focus on Decentralized Applications (Dapps) and their integral role in the DeFi ecosystem.

What is DeFi?

DeFi, short for Decentralized Finance, refers to a broad category of financial applications and services that are built on blockchain networks. Unlike traditional financial systems that rely on centralized intermediaries such as banks and brokerages, DeFi operates on a decentralized network of nodes using the concept of smart contracts. These smart contracts are self-executing contracts with the terms of the agreement directly written into code. This decentralization removes the need for intermediaries, reducing costs and increasing accessibility. DeFi encompasses a wide range of services, including lending and borrowing platforms, decentralized exchanges (DEXs), stablecoins, and insurance protocols.

What are Dapps?

Dapps, or decentralized applications, are apps that run on blockchain networks instead of traditional servers. They are a key part of Decentralized Finance (DeFi), allowing people to access financial services without going through banks or other middlemen. This makes things more transparent, secure, and easy to access. For example, Dapps can be used for trading cryptocurrencies, borrowing and lending money, and creating automated financial services, all helping to make finance more open and fair for everyone.

Principles

The theory behind DeFi is rooted in the principles of decentralization, transparency, and inclusivity. At its core, DeFi aims to eliminate the inefficiencies and inequities of traditional financial systems. Key elements of DeFi include:

Decentralization: Utilizing blockchain technology to ensure transactions are not controlled by any single entity.

Transparency: Ensuring that transactions are transparent, immutable, and verifiable by anyone, builds trust and reduces the risk of fraud.

Inclusivity: Providing access to financial services to anyone with an internet connection, regardless of their location or socio-economic status.

Open-Source Innovation: Allowing continuous innovation and collaboration within the community, fostering a dynamic and rapidly evolving ecosystem.

Key Components

Several key components underpin the DeFi ecosystem. These include:

Smart Contracts: These are self-executing contracts with the agreement terms directly written into code, facilitating automated and trustless transactions.

Decentralized Exchanges (DEXs): Platforms that enable users to trade cryptocurrencies directly with one another without intermediaries.

Stablecoins: Cryptocurrencies pegged to stable assets like fiat currencies, reducing volatility and providing a stable medium of exchange.

Lending and Borrowing Protocols: Platforms that allow users to lend their assets to earn interest or borrow assets by providing collateral.

Liquidity Pools: Pools of tokens provided by users to facilitate trading on DEXs, often in exchange for a share of transaction fees.

Use Case Segment

Case Study: Lido Finance

Lido Finance is a leading, large-scale DeFi protocol specializing in liquid staking solutions, operating globally. It enables users to stake their Ethereum (ETH) and receive stETH tokens in return. These stETH tokens represent the staked ETH and can be actively used in various DeFi applications. This allows users to earn staking rewards while maintaining liquidity. Revenue is generated through staking rewards and transaction fees, benefiting participants such as DeFi users, Ethereum stakes, validators, and developers.

Problem

Traditional Staking: Requires users to lock up their assets, reducing liquidity and flexibility in asset management.

Centralized Staking Solutions: Pose security risks and can lead to inefficiencies in the decentralized ecosystem.

Solution

Lido Finance addresses these issues by providing a liquid staking solution that offers:

Enhanced Liquidity: Users receive stETH tokens, which can be used in DeFi applications while still earning staking rewards.

Decentralized Security: Reducing reliance on centralized staking services, thereby enhancing security and efficiency within the ecosystem.

Advantages

Liquidity: One of the primary benefits of Lido Finance is the liquidity it provides. By receiving stETH tokens, users can access and utilize their staked assets without needing to lock them up. This flexibility is a significant advantage for users who want to participate in other DeFi activities while still earning staking rewards.

Earnings: Lido Finance allows users to continue earning staking rewards on their staked ETH. These rewards accumulate over time, providing an additional income stream while users leverage their stETH in other DeFi protocols.

Security: The security of Lido Finance is bolstered by its decentralized network of validators. This decentralization reduces the risks associated with centralization and enhances the overall security of the staking process.

Challenges

Smart Contract Risk: Like all DeFi protocols, Lido Finance is not immune to the risks associated with smart contracts. There is always an inherent risk of vulnerabilities within the code, which could potentially be exploited by malicious actors.

Price Fluctuations: The value of stETH can fluctuate relative to ETH. If the peg between stETH and ETH is not maintained, users might face potential losses, adding a layer of financial risk to the staking process.

Complexity: Liquid staking, while advantageous, comes with its complexities. Users need to have a thorough understanding of how liquid staking works and be aware of the associated risks to make informed decisions.

ExO Attributes

Staff on Demand: Utilizes a decentralized network of validators.
Community & Crowd: Engages the DeFi community for participation and development.
Leveraged Assets: Users' staked ETH generates continuous staking rewards.
Decentralization: Enhances security and reduces risks associated with centralization.

OKRs/KPIs

Objective: Increase the total value staked (TVS) by 20% within six months.
Key Indicator: Total value of ETH staked on the platform.
Objective: Achieve a 95% peg stability between stETH and ETH.
Key Indicator: Peg stability ratio.
Objective: Expand user base by 30% in the next quarter.
Key Indicator: Number of active users and new users.

Approach

Development: Built and deployed the liquid staking protocol on Ethereum.

Security: Conducted extensive smart contract audits and engaged in continuous security monitoring.

Community Engagement: Held educational webinars and created detailed guides to inform users about liquid staking.

Lessons Learned

The importance of thorough smart contract audits to mitigate risks.
The a need for user education to ensure users understand liquid staking and associated risks.
The challenge of maintaining the peg between stETH and ETH requires continuous monitoring and adjustment.

Looking Forward

Continuous improvement of the protocol based on user feedback.
Ongoing security assessments and updates.
Expanding to support the staking of additional cryptocurrencies.

Lido Finance illustrates the innovative potential of DeFi protocols in providing flexible and secure financial solutions. As the DeFi ecosystem evolves, protocols like Lido Finance will play a crucial role in shaping the future of decentralized financial services.

Case Study: MakerDAO

MakerDAO is a pioneering DeFi protocol that addresses the instability of the cryptocurrency market by facilitating the creation of the DAI stablecoin, which is pegged to the US dollar. Operating on the Ethereum blockchain, MakerDAO allows users to lock up collateral in the form of various cryptocurrencies to generate DAI. This decentralized approach to stablecoins provides a stable and secure medium of exchange, mitigating the risks associated with traditional, centralized stablecoins.

Problem

Cryptocurrency Volatility: The inherent volatility of cryptocurrencies makes it challenging for users to find a stable medium of exchange and store of value.

Centralization Risks: Traditional stablecoins often rely on central entities, which introduces risks of centralization and trust issues.

Solution

Stable Medium of Exchange: DAI provides a stable medium of exchange within the volatile cryptocurrency market.

Decentralized Approach: By allowing users to lock up collateral in various cryptocurrencies, MakerDAO eliminates the need for central entities, reducing centralization risks and trust issues.

Advantages

Stability: The primary advantage of MakerDAO is the stability it provides through DAI. By pegging DAI to the US dollar, MakerDAO offers a reliable and stable currency that can be used for transactions, savings, and DeFi activities without the typical volatility associated with cryptocurrencies.

Decentralization: MakerDAO is governed by a decentralized community of MKR token holders who vote on key decisions, such as adjustments to collateralization ratios and other protocol parameters. This decentralized governance model enhances transparency and reduces the risks of centralization.

Flexibility: MakerDAO supports multiple types of collateral, including other cryptocurrencies such as ETH, BAT, and USDC, among others. This flexibility allows users to leverage a variety of assets to generate DAI, catering to diverse financial needs and strategies.

Challenges

Collateralization Risk: Users must over-collateralize their loans to generate DAI, meaning they need to lock up more value in collateral than the amount of DAI they receive. If the value of the collateral drops significantly, users risk liquidation, where their collateral is sold to cover the debt.

Complexity: Engaging with MakerDAO requires a solid understanding of the mechanics of over-collateralization, liquidation, and the governance process. This complexity can be a barrier for new users or those unfamiliar with DeFi concepts.

Governance Risks: While decentralized governance is a strength, it also poses risks. Disagreements among MKR holders or poorly informed decisions can impact the stability and security of the protocol.

ExO Attributes

Decentralization: Governance by MKR token holders ensures decisions are made collectively.

Autonomy: Smart contracts automate the issuance and management of DAI.

Social Technologies: Community governance and voting mechanisms.

Algorithms: Collateralization and liquidation processes are automated via smart contracts.

OKRs/KPIs

Objective: Maintain the stability of DAI
Key Indicator: Keep DAI price close to $1.
Objective: Increase user adoption and collateral types
Key Indicator: Expand supported collateral types.
Objective: Ensure robust governance participation
Key Indicator: Increase the number of active MKR voters.

Approach

Implement a robust smart contract system on Ethereum, allowing users to lock collateral and generate DAI. The protocol introduced a governance token (MKR) to decentralize decision-making and apply stability fees and liquidation penalties to provide revenue and help maintain the peg to the US dollar.

Lessons Learned

Importance of User Education: The complexity of MakerDAO's system requires thorough user education to prevent mismanagement of collateral.

Governance Challenges: Decentralized governance can be slow and contentious, highlighting the need for effective community coordination.

Risk Management: Over-collateralization is crucial to protect against price volatility and ensure system stability.

Looking Forward

continuously evolves by integrating new collateral types
improving governance mechanisms
enhancing user interfaces to simplify interaction
Ongoing audits and updates ensure the security and reliability of the protocol

MakerDAO represents a cornerstone of the DeFi ecosystem by providing a decentralized and stable currency in the form of DAI. Its decentralized governance and support for multiple types of collateral make it a versatile and resilient protocol.

Case Study: Rocket Pool

Rocket Pool is a decentralized Ethereum 2.0 staking protocol designed to make staking more accessible and decentralized. It allows users to stake their ETH and participate in Ethereum's proof-of-stake network without needing to meet the minimum requirement of 32 ETH. By providing a decentralized staking pool, Rocket Pool enables smaller stakeholders to contribute to network security and earn staking rewards. With over 3,500+ node operators across 145+ regions, Rocket Pool helps stake 700,000+ ETH.

Problem

High Entry Barrier: Traditional Ethereum 2.0 staking requires a minimum of 32 ETH, which is a significant barrier for many potential stakes.

Centralization Risks: Centralized staking solutions pose risks related to security and control, potentially undermining the decentralized ethos of Ethereum.

Solution

Lowering the Entry Barrier: Allowing users to stake any amount of ETH, making staking more accessible to a broader audience.

Ensuring Decentralization: Offering a decentralized platform that mitigates risks associated with centralized staking, enhancing security and adherence to Ethereum's decentralized principles.

Advantages

Accessibility: Rocket Pool lowers the barrier to entry for Ethereum staking by allowing users to stake with as little as 0.01 ETH. This accessibility democratizes participation in Ethereum's proof-of-stake network, enabling more users to contribute to network security and earn rewards.

Decentralization: Rocket Pool employs a network of decentralized node operators who manage the staking process. This decentralization enhances security and reduces the risks associated with centralized staking services.

Flexibility: Users can stake their ETH and receive rETH tokens in return. These rETH tokens represent the staked ETH and can be used in other DeFi protocols, providing liquidity and flexibility similar to the stETH tokens in Lido Finance.

Challenges

Smart Contract Risk: As with other DeFi protocols, Rocket Pool relies on smart contracts to manage staking and reward distribution. These smart contracts are subject to potential vulnerabilities that could be exploited by malicious actors.

Price Fluctuations: The value of rETH can fluctuate relative to ETH, which may lead to potential losses if the peg is not maintained. Users must be aware of this risk when staking through Rocket Pool.

Complexity: Understanding how Rocket Pool operates, including the roles of node operators and the mechanics of rETH, can be complex for new users. Adequate education and understanding are necessary to navigate these complexities effectively.

ExO Attributes

Decentralization: Uses decentralized node operators to manage staking.

Accessibility: Lowers staking entry requirements to 0.01 ETH.

Liquidity: Provides rETH tokens that can be used in other DeFi protocols.

Security: Smart contracts are audited to ensure safety and reliability.

OKRs/KPIs

Objective: Increase in total ETH staked
Indicator: Total ETH staked over a specified period
Objective: Number of active node operators.
Indicator: Number of active node operators
Objective: Enhance User Adoption and Growth
Indicator: Growth rate of unique stakes

Objective: Boost rETH Token Utilization in DeFi

Indicator: Volume and frequency of rETH token utilization within DeFi protocols

Approach

Rocket Pool launched with a focus on decentralizing the staking process by recruiting a network of node operators. The platform underwent extensive smart contract audits to ensure security. Marketing efforts targeted Ethereum holders and DeFi enthusiasts, emphasizing the low staking threshold and the flexibility of rETH tokens.

Lessons Learned

Education is crucial: Users need comprehensive guides and support to understand the staking process and the use of rETH tokens.

Continuous audits are necessary: Regular security audits are essential to maintain trust and mitigate smart contract risks.

Market volatility management: Ensuring that rETH maintains a stable peg to ETH is vital for user confidence.

Looking Forward

Rocket Pool plans to expand its node operator network and enhance its educational resources for users. The team is also exploring partnerships with other DeFi protocols to increase the utility of rETH tokens.

Rocket Pool stands out as an innovative solution in the Ethereum staking space, providing greater accessibility, decentralization, and flexibility. By addressing the challenges of traditional staking and offering unique benefits, it supports a more inclusive and robust Ethereum proof-of-stake ecosystem.

Democratization in Action

One of the most profound impacts of DeFi is its role in democratizing access to financial services. Traditional financial systems often exclude individuals due to geographic, economic, or regulatory barriers. DeFi, by contrast, is accessible to anyone with an internet connection, allowing individuals in underserved regions to access financial products and services. This democratization empowers individuals, promotes financial inclusion, and can drive economic growth in developing regions. Furthermore, the open-source nature of DeFi encourages innovation and collaboration, allowing for the continuous development of new and improved financial solutions that can benefit a global user base.

For instance, Lido Finance allows users to stake with any amount of ETH, providing stETH as a liquid representation of staked assets. MakerDAO enables anyone to generate DAI stablecoins by locking crypto assets in smart contracts, governed by a decentralized community. Similarly, Rocket Pool permits staking with as little as 0.01 ETH, issuing rETH tokens that can be utilized in the broader DeFi ecosystem.

Applying DeFi to an Organization

For a financial organization, integrating Decentralized Finance (DeFi) can bring several benefits, increased efficiency, cost savings, and improved security. Here are some areas to explore and steps to initiate the integration of DeFi:

Assess Fit

Current Processes: Examine your organization's current financial processes, such as lending, borrowing, and asset management. Identify areas where DeFi can streamline operations.

Customer Needs: Consider how DeFi can meet the evolving needs of your customers by offering more flexible and accessible financial products.

Benefits

Efficiency: DeFi can automate and simplify financial processes, reducing the need for intermediaries and cutting associated fees.

Security: The transparency and immutability of blockchain transactions can enhance security and reduce the risk of fraud.

Cost Reduction: Lower operational costs by eliminating middlemen and improving transaction speed and accuracy.

Initiating Steps

Research DeFi Protocols: Start by exploring various DeFi protocols relevant to your business needs, such as decentralized lending platforms or asset management tools.

Pilot Projects: Implement small-scale pilot projects to test the effectiveness and feasibility of DeFi solutions within your organization.

Partnerships: Consider partnering with existing DeFi platforms to leverage their expertise and technology.

Regulatory Compliance: Ensure that any DeFi integration complies with current financial regulations to mitigate potential legal risks.

Moving Forward

Training and Education: Educate your team about DeFi and its potential impact on your organization.

Customer Communication: Inform your customers about the new DeFi-based services and how they can benefit from them.

Feedback and Iteration: Collect feedback from both employees and customers to refine and improve the DeFi integration.

By taking these steps, your organization can begin its journey toward becoming an exponential organization, leveraging DeFi to enhance operations and deliver better financial services.

Conclusion

DeFi represents a paradigm shift in the way financial services are conceived and delivered. By leveraging blockchain technology and smart contracts, DeFi offers a decentralized, transparent, and inclusive alternative to traditional financial systems. Decentralized Applications (Dapps) play a crucial role in this ecosystem, providing the infrastructure and tools necessary for DeFi to function effectively. While there are challenges and risks associated with DeFi, the potential benefits, such as increased accessibility, reduced costs, and enhanced security, make it a compelling area of innovation. As financial organizations explore the integration of DeFi solutions, they must navigate the regulatory landscape carefully to harness the full potential of this transformative technology.

Appendix: Sources

Internet resources

Lido Finance Official Documentation. https://docs.lido.fi/
MakerDAO Official Documentation.
https://docs.makerdao.com/
MakerDAO Community. https://community-development.makerdao.com/
Rocket Pool Official Documentation.
https://docs.rocketpool.net/
Rocket Pool Overview. https://medium.com/rocket-pool

World Economic Forum Report on DeFi. https://www.weforum.org/reports/decentralized-finance-defi-policy-maker-toolkit

Ethereum Foundation Blog. https://blog.ethereum.org/

Publications

Ismael, S., Malone, M. S., & van Geest, Y. (Year of Publication). Exponential Organizations 2.0: Why New Organizations Are Ten Times Better, Faster, and Cheaper Than Yours (and What to Do About It). Publisher Name.

Contact Rob Bassani

https://www.linkedin.com/in/rob-bassani-0a915920/

CHAPTER 11
REGENERATIVE ARCHITECTURE: DISRUPTING THE $17 TRILLION CONSTRUCTION INDUSTRY

STACEY MURPHY

Multi-Transformative Purpose: To help people awaken to their true nature.

Earthshot: To cultivate biologically alive buildings that grow, regenerate, and compost themselves so that cities harmonize with nature, enhance biodiversity, and restore ecosystems.

Why Grow Buildings?

The architecture and construction industries are ripe for change. They could do a lot better to help provide clean water, energy, air, and food for all.

We've got some challenges to address. Not only is the construction industry responsible for 39% of greenhouse gas emissions, but it is also the leader in ecosystem destruction and deforestation leading to biodiversity loss and extinction. Construction waste accounts for 25-30% of all waste generated which further contributes to pollution and environmental degradation. Construction activities also consume large quantities of water and often lead to water pollution. The construction sector's demand for water can lead to the depletion of local water sources, impacting both ecosystems and human communities.

It's definitely time to do things differently.
In a nutshell, how did we get here?

Modern cities, products of the Industrial Era, were conceptualized much like machines. This era focused on separation: it compartmentalized living from working, hid sewage and landfills far from public view, and divided the financial pursuits in real estate from the philanthropic efforts in public works. Most critically, it made nature separate from humans and saw it as a resource to be extracted rather than integrated.

Today, fortunately, more people today are realizing that everything is connected. It is not too late to reconnect the dots and restore the Earth's precious life support systems while simultaneously expanding the economy through innovative markets. There's a win-win-win scenario within reach that positively benefits our planet.

Business today is characterized by an unprecedented level of collaboration. This enables us to tackle these multifaceted challenges from various angles, ensuring more comprehensive solutions.

The belief that man-made machines are more efficient than nature still lingers, but more and more people are appreciating the power of cooperation, which is the power of nature.

Since everything is connected, nature-based solutions tend to improve everything, everywhere, all at once. They work faster than you might realize.

Nature regenerates and evolves. That is the essence of Regenerative Design. As the principles of Regenerative Design are applied to cities and infrastructure, the effects will be otherworldly.

In this chapter, you'll discover:

Three regenerative principles that are redefining cities and infrastructure.

What the architecture and construction industries will look like by 2030 and the timeline to get there.

The emerging market opportunities and the pioneering startups poised to capitalize on these developments.

What is Regenerative?

Regenerative goes beyond sustainability. The words are not interchangeable.

Nature is not a steady-state equation to be solved and optimized like a machine. Nature evolves, expands, and adapts. This is the primary difference between the concepts of sustainability and regeneration.

Sustainability is our human desire for things to be quantifiable and, measurable… essentially to sustain the systems that we currently have without depleting them for future generations, reducing harm, and minimizing resource use.

Regeneration is about encouraging more life to thrive, enriching interactions within nature, and rejuvenating ecosystems.

When applied to architecture, sustainability is optimizing the glass on a building to reduce energy consumption. Regenerative is reimagining a material that might look like glass, but that regenerates on a cellular level to adapt to its environment all while delivering energy to the building.

Sustainability is settling for balancing the Earth's temperatures to not exceed the tipping point. Regenerative is knowing that we can restore our ecosystems to pre-industrial era temperatures AND improve the quality of life at the same time.

Sustainability is accepting larger climate events as inevitable and feeling fearful and powerless against nature. Regenerative is knowing that we are evolving and can choose to be MORE in harmony with nature instead of at odds.

Embracing the Regenerative Mindset

Regeneration is a biological term, but it's more than that. It's also a gateway to possibilities that defy conventional limits. What are some concrete examples of regeneration in nature and what would it mean to apply those principles to city infrastructure?

The axolotl is the poster child for regeneration. If you cut off a limb, it is capable of reconstructing the entire limb, bone and all, in 40 days. It can reverse heart, brain, and spinal cord injuries within days as well. That's fast!

Imagine harnessing this phenomenal natural ability in our buildings and cities.

Picture the room around you. It's fundamentally a container, holding the same air you breathe. But what if the boundaries of this room were more than static barriers? Imagine if the walls around you were breathing and transforming.

Sounds a bit like your lungs or diaphragm perhaps.

In your body, your stomach is the hero of regeneration. The acid in your stomach eats the entire lining every 2-9 days, but your stomach never leaks because the cells regenerate themselves just as quickly. Now imagine this is the room you are sitting in… minus the acid of course.

From your body to entire forests, nature has this inherent capacity to regenerate. That's what it does when we allow it. That's what being a steward means, to allow nature to thrive.

Facing significant impacts of environmental degradation – a legacy of the Industrial Era's dominance over nature – a pivotal question arises. What if we approached infrastructure development not just as builders, but as stewards, actively nurturing living ecosystems?

If the Industrial Era has chopped off a limb so to speak, how fast might we restore, rejuvenate, and regenerate Earth's ecosystems with a Regenerative Mindset?

The Roots of Regenerative Architecture

Embracing the Regenerative Mindset is not just the future, it's a rich part of indigenous wisdom. Exploring the mysteries of ancient construction challenges our bias toward permanence and security and unlocks new possibilities.

Consider the Q'eswachaka bridge in Peru. This grass-woven bridge has spanned the Apurímac River canyon for centuries. How has grass withstood as a building material for that long? It seems counterintuitive that such delicate grass could create a structure robust enough to endure centuries of use.

The Q'eswachaka bridge is rebuilt annually by the community. This is continuity through renewal. You can count on this bridge being there: the concept is permanent, but the object is renewable.

Imagine applying this concept to city infrastructure. What if buildings could be renewed and regenerated regularly, like the Q'eswachaka bridge? Instead of resisting change, structures could adapt to shifting needs, environmental conditions, and emerging advancements.

It might sound wasteful. Afterall, isn't durability a part of sustainability? Compostable, biologically alive materials could be the key to restoring local soil and ecosystems while allowing us to alter the fabric of our lives.

This could be really helpful when you realize how much demolition there is of outdated buildings. Remodeling and "spring cleaning" would be an ongoing, seamless process.

What if we enlisted the help of robots to weave building materials together and sensors to measure in-the-moment structural stability? There might be a blending of regenerative materials and machines that will allow this indigenous practice to evolve.

Taking it one step further, there are living root bridges in India where the people have mastered the art of guiding aerial roots of rubber fig trees across rivers and gorges using bamboo scaffolding. These bridges have lasted centuries and are still living and growing. Some of them are double high.

Imagine how the ancient art of building with living materials, augmented by modern robotics and sensors, could transform the way we design and construct our cities.

If you're already questioning all the challenges including construction schedules, consider the opportunities of 3D printed scaffolding that allows the living structure to fill in more quickly. More on that in later sections.

The future is weird. But so is our ancient history.

There remain mysteries around the ancient pyramids all around the world. It's not just about the plant kingdom, what about those giant mineral and crystalline structures? The pyramids stand as a testament to a pearl of ancient wisdom, possibly hinting at uses of natural energy that modern science has yet to rediscover or understand fully.

Redefining Architecture as Regenerative

Your imagination might already be buzzing; here are some more groundbreaking ideas to consider as we redefine architecture to be truly regenerative.

Imagine:

- Buildings growing themselves and shedding parts they no longer need.
- Surfaces regenerate to adapt to changing environmental conditions.
- Walls that shift colors based on your preferences throughout the day.

- Rooms that don't box you in and are shaped more like nests, trees, or ponds.
- Geometries that harmonize your body in the frequency of vitality.
- Materials that change texture add aesthetic and sensory experiences.
- Nature-based systems that recycle, purify, and remineralize your water.
- Bio-based materials generate more than enough power for everyone.
- Molten memory metals and crystals that phase change for quicker reconstruction.
- Homes that generate income for inhabitants in a vibrant, nature-based market.
- Ecosystems of interconnected buildings with bank accounts.
- Bioregions granted legal rights to receive financial contributions from real estate developments that use locally sourced materials
- Robotic insects that evaluate infrastructure, inform future material adjustments and make repairs as necessary

This might all sound a bit wild, and undoubtedly, it raises many questions. Is this science fiction?

You might be surprised at how close we are to making this futuristic vision a reality, and how quickly nature can accelerate our progress. Futurists often emphasize exponential technologies as catalysts for human expansion, but they frequently underestimate the powerful role that nature-based solutions play in achieving our global environmental goals and their investment potential.

Nature as the Original Open-Source Exponential Technology

When you think of exponential technologies, your mind might leap to innovations like the internet, AI, robotics, or advanced sensors—man-made marvels that enable rapid growth. But what if the original exponential technology has been thriving for billions of years, right under our noses? Enter Nature's Intelligence (NI), the oldest and most sophisticated technology on the planet.

You're likely familiar with regenerative buzzwords such as circular economies, swarm behavior, hive mind, systems thinking, ecosystem services, biomimicry, and biodiversity. These strategies aren't new. You may also know some of the design tactics of these strategies – being adaptive, resilient, renewable, holistic, anticipatory, syntropic, fractal, and decentralized.

But underlying all these outward strategies and tactics are underlying regenerative principles.

A lot of the strategies and tactics can be applied metaphorically.

Let's go beyond the metaphor that our buildings are LIKE flowers.

What if our buildings ARE flowers?

If we are to truly transcend traditional architecture and develop buildings and infrastructure that are not just inspired by nature but are living entities themselves, we've got to think differently.

In order to innovate, focus on first principles, straight from the source.

Get ready! These three regenerative principles are going to stretch your comfort zone.

Principle 1: Emergence

Nature's Intelligence is an open-source platform where the code of life – DNA – is freely shared and continuously evolving. Each species contributes to and benefits from this vast, interconnected web of life.

Every day, new species are discovered. That's one form of emergence, new discoveries. In 2023, scientists estimated that 86% of Earth's species are still unknown.

DNA gets wilder than that. There's an even more powerful form of emergence that happens every day.

It's easy to see in a garden. Picture bumblebees as tiny messengers, buzzing from one blossom to another, mixing and mingling DNA among the squash, cucumber, and melon flowers as they go. Thanks to their busy work, new types of fruits emerge from nature's cross-pollinating creativity.

But much more emerges from intermingling DNA than meets the eye.

Dr. Konstantin Meyl has demonstrated that the double-helix DNA functions much like a radio tower. According to his study, DNA can send and receive information using a type of energy similar to light waves, which he refers to as magnetic solar waves. These signals create harmony or resonance, not just within the body but across the universe, using what he calls 'scalar energy' as a means to transmit signals.

This represents a paradigm shift in how we understand and interact with the natural world, moving beyond chemical and physical interactions to include electromagnetic, frequency, and informational interactions as fundamental processes.

Since humans see only 0.003% of the electromagnetic spectrum and we only hear between 20 Hz - 20,000 Hz, there's a lot more being shared via DNA than our primary senses allow us to understand.

What DNA information might be shared as we inhabit buildings that are actively growing and sentient? What will we learn about our own nature as DNA expands in this relationship?

What opportunities will emerge on this new frontier of our human consciousness?

How might we cross-pollinate with living buildings?

Principle 2: Biology is Quantum

You might think biology is too messy to be quantum because quantum physics is about particles in laboratories.

But those plants you see in your garden are actually quantum computers.

Photosynthesis is known for transforming carbon dioxide and sunlight into sugar and oxygen. What most people don't know is that the first step of photosynthesis is the most efficient energy transformation process on the planet. Nearly 100% of photon energy from the Sun is converted into electron energy for sugar production. How? Quantum coherence and quantum tunneling enable this remarkable efficiency.

Human designs rarely achieve even half this efficiency.

Physicists have been able to achieve close to 100% efficiency only under extreme conditions like near absolute zero, with lasers, or superconductivity. In photosynthesis, however, it happens in the wet and wild environments of plants.

Why is this important to the fields of architecture and construction?

Wouldn't it be helpful to crack the code on decentralized, scalable energy?

Want lighter, stronger, more flexible structures? Quantum materials make the most of the natural strengths found in atoms and molecules.

Plus, quantum materials exhibit exotic behaviors like changing phase, superconductivity, magnetoresistance, and coherence. Quantum materials could revolutionize environmental monitoring by changing colors and patterns to indicate shifts in Earth's conditions, providing a visually intuitive way to track ecological changes.

Biology is quantum and it's weird. As stewards of Nature's Intelligence, it's worth a trip down the rabbit hole, because it will change how we build infrastructure in quantum leaps. Which is exactly what we need to restore, rejuvenate, and regenerate quickly.

Principle 3: Honoring All LIfe

What would it mean to truly honor all life? At first, this question may seem abstract and idealistic, but it is precisely this principle that will pave the way for trillions of dollars in emerging markets from which more people can benefit.

Consider a single cherry tomato plant. From one tiny seed, the plant produces hundreds of tomatoes, each tomato has another ten seeds, potentially seeding thousands of new plants. Animals and birds eat the tomatoes, disperse the seeds through their droppings, and new plants spring up far and wide. This illustrates the exponential growth potential inherent in nature.

But what fuels this expansion?

You might credit the billions of microorganisms in the soil that fed the plant nutrients, the glacier that deposited those nutrients thousands of years ago, or maybe the fungi that spread important messages from plant to plant. But what about the water and the sunlight? You get the point.

Everything in the ecosystem is exchanging energy much like a stock market, contributing to what you might call nature's capital.

Honoring all life means valuing all those energy exchanges as a shared equity system.

Scientists refer to energy exchange as thermodynamics. The more nodes you connect, the more energy is exchanged, and the more value is created. Turns out the value increases exponentially as the network grows.

How might this principle be applied to our city infrastructure?

The fastest place to start is to look at the most undervalued things and reclaim their value.

Here's where it gets a little weird.

What if you got paid to poop, but only if you use a compost toilet that feeds the landscape? Isn't it odd that we buy composted cow manure for our gardens and yet flush our waste down the toilet, turning it into "solid waste" and using approximately 3.5 billion gallons of water daily in wastewater treatment systems?

Designing a city from scratch would look much different today. But there is an immediate opportunity to unlock the value of bioregional financing and nature-based assets that would incentivize better quality air, water, food, and energy.

What new financial instruments will emerge for trading ecosystem services of buildings and infrastructure?

Valuable: Catalyzing Emerging Markets

In traditional architecture, the value of a property has been narrowly defined by its potential for human habitation and its physical assets. This perspective overlooks a crucial dimension: the potential for buildings to act as vibrant ecosystems providing a multitude of services—restoring habitats, purifying air and water, and generating energy. If we reframe buildings as biologically alive entities, maybe they have their own bank accounts.

Cities benefit from the network effect of many buildings sharing resources.

One example of this in action is how Except Studios helped to create the SalesForce Park, a public 5.4-acre rooftop park. How was it funded? They talked to all the neighboring properties about the appreciation of their real estate value with the addition of the park, and they paid that future appreciation to have the park built for their collective good.

Community solar is another way groups of buildings have come together to act as an ecosystem for win-win solutions around financing the future they want.

This only scratches the surface of what is possible.

Let's look at an example that could create another income stream for cities. In 2009, my think tank produced FarmShare, an award-winning project that transformed undervalued urban spaces and city resources into a thriving decentralized local food system. A lot of people thought we were a farm and underestimated our value. The secret sauce was an open-source platform, enabling tens of thousands of people to participate. Farm managers listed activities and bounties. Participants listed their available resources and matched them with their desired bounties.

The more people joined, the more products and bounties were available which brought more people to participate.

This system illustrated the power of network effects in amplifying value. For example, one participant with a station wagon and a few hours to spare each week collected three dozen eggs from the coop; then gathered chaff from the coffee roaster for chicken bedding and spent grains from the brewery for chicken feed. In the process, he distributed eggs to each vendor and enjoyed tasty, new products from these local businesses. This not only reduced operating costs for the farm and all the vendors who would have had to pay disposal fees but also enhanced the participant's feeling of ownership in the kinds of rewards that meant the most to him.

For a fun two hours in the urban farm ecosystem, he received his dozen eggs, six packs of beer, and a bag of fresh coffee beans.

Cooperation increases value across the whole network.
The more nodes you connect, the more value is created.

In 2010 we were trying to tokenize so we could measure this value in one metric, but we ran into technology hurdles and burnt out.

Today's world is much different with new opportunities to measure these values.

Except Studio has an Orchid City concept which shows if we built a city of 50,000 and did nothing different other than network them together to share resources that we could save 140% on our carbon footprint per person, and contribute billions in jobs, all while restoring biodiversity and habitat.

Now imagine including regenerative materials and systems in the mix.

Currently, the concrete and steel markets dominate the construction landscape with projected growths reaching approximately USD 822 Billion and USD 1.3 Trillion by 2026 and 2030, respectively. Concrete and steel are also the largest contributors to CO_2 emissions within the industry which makes them a primary target for disruption. There are dozens of startups (maybe even hundreds by the time you read this) focused on concrete alone.

Replacing an established system can take some time to reduce the price point to one that is comparable, especially if costs have been externalized already.

To address this, what if an ecosystem of buildings decided to share the investment of testing a new material in exchange for equity in the product? This would incentivize more innovation in the industry overall.

How much economic potential could be unlocked when allowing buildings and bioregions to be exchanged?

The Timeline: Regenerative Architecture by 2030

You're probably wondering, is growing buildings by 2030 even possible?

Well, it's going to take an ecosystem.

The current system of architecture as a service industry isn't going to move fast enough to reach global goals set forth by the United Nations SDGs, The Paris Agreement, and Net Zero commitments. Site-specific projects with timelines and budgets are not conducive environments for innovation.

It's time for cooperation across the industry.

What if you were part of an ecosystem where you helped design new products and services to be used globally and you were rewarded with shared equity?

That's the mission of Dreaming Earth. It is an architectural impact studio that cultivates a professional network of regenerative visionaries, scientists, and investors; facilitates new product teams, incubates startups; and connects investors. Memberships are available at the professional and enterprise level where your company receives training and continuing education credits. This innovative model shifts the industry paradigm from hourly-wage service providers to a dynamic, equity-sharing ecosystem, empowering teams to drive meaningful change and share in the success.

The first Earthshot of Dreaming Earth is to cultivate regenerative buildings by 2030. Here's the timeline of innovation and market readiness with action steps.

2025: Network of Regenerative Community Stakeholders

Cultivate a network of stakeholders including architects, biologists, engineers, urban planners, local governments, investors, and community organizations to foster interdisciplinary collaboration.

Educate the public and key industry players about the benefits and processes involved in regenerative architecture to build support and participation.

Form strategic partnerships with academic institutions, research centers, innovation hubs, and private sector players to drive innovation and resource sharing.

Develop open-source platforms where ideas, designs, research findings, and best practices can be shared globally.

Engage with policymakers to begin shaping the legal and regulatory framework that will support regenerative building practices.

2026-2027: Integration & Expansion

Implement pilot projects in various climates to demonstrate the viability and benefits of regenerative systems.

Validate the structural integrity of regenerative technologies and gather data to support regulatory changes. Testing of different aspects in growing buildings to provide clean water, energy, and food for all.

Establish market incentives for businesses and homeowners to invest in regenerative buildings, such as tax breaks, subsidies, and enhanced ecosystem service credits.

Expand outreach to gather input and foster public-private partnerships that encourage industry adoption of regenerative projects.

Scale up successful pilot projects to larger developments to test the practicality of broader implementation.

2028-2029: Standardization & Commercialization

Begin large-scale construction projects utilizing regenerative technologies. Promote commercialization through incentives and subsidies.

Implement standardized methods for valuing, tracking, and trading the ecosystem services generated by regenerative buildings.

Ensure that supply chains are established for the widespread distribution of regenerative materials.

2030: Cultivating LIVE Buildings

Goal: New buildings capable of self-regeneration, integrated with nature, fully recyclable and/or compostable.

Who's Leading the Way?

As the architecture and construction industries evolve, a new wave of startups and visionaries is reshaping the future with groundbreaking materials and building systems. From growing the building blocks of tomorrow to using robotics for repurposing lumber, these pioneers are taking the first steps needed to create new economies.

It makes sense that before we grow entire buildings, we grow regenerative building blocks that replace existing products. These building blocks have the ability to restore ecosystems, and sequester carbon and they are completely compostable, unlike the existing options. Innovation labs in mushrooms, algae, and hemp are reimagining how a building positively changes the planet. These are some of the fastest-growing substances on the planet, but they will face challenges to scale for mass adoption.

Mushrooms are some of the largest organisms in the world. In the mushroom world is Blast Studio. They are 3D printing using coffee filters and infusing them with mycelium to test structural mushroom columns. This complements existing products like mushroom insulation and chairs.

Some species of kelp can grow up to two feet per day. Kelp Island is making strides with its patented SeaBrick which could soon replace marine concrete. The brilliance of Kelp Island lies in its focus on expanding its own supply chain. They are developing products that will enable the construction and scaling of dense, floating kelp forests in the ocean. The more they produce, the more is possible for them to produce. Their projections show that they could sequester enough carbon by 2050 to get us back to pre-Industrial Era levels.

Hemp is the fastest-growing plant in temperate climates. When it comes to hemp, most people think of hempcrete, but this industry is expanding quickly. Hemp farmers are revolutionizing the industry by designing a comprehensive system of architectural components ranging from hemp rebar to hemp piping (an alternative to PVC) and hemp 4'x8' boards to replace plywood. The benefits of using hemp are extensive—from local soil improvement and carbon sequestration to preventing erosion. Hemp rebar, in particular, offers an alternative to steel rebar, one of the most carbon-intensive materials in construction. It enhances the durability of roads by preventing corrosion and reduces energy consumption in buildings by eliminating thermal bridging.

Beyond growing new products, another great first step is to use robotics to help create more circular economies in the industry. A growing number of robotic startups like Urban Machine are making significant contributions. The primary obstacle in repurposing lumber is metal fasteners. Urban Machine has a robotic solution that senses and removes these metal fasteners allowing for the lumber to be reused. This is revolutionizing how architects specify the deconstruction of buildings at the end of the life cycle.

Water and energy are going to see significant innovation in the coming years. Builders and developers need adaptable, flexible, decentralized infrastructure for the new kinds of homes they are building. LeapFrog Design is a nature-based solution to treat and reuse water. Estuary is a modular planter box that treats your gray water for non-potable reuse in toilet flushing or irrigation. Regenerative energy solutions are coming, too, and they are going to be weird and wonderful.

This is just a taste of what's to come.

It's ALIVE!

If it's hard to imagine what a day-in-the-life would be like when buildings actually grow themselves, you're not alone.

It can be tricky to understand all the ripple effects of what this will mean for civilization.

As we contemplate buildings that are living organisms, we are not just rethinking architecture. We are redefining our responsibilities and capabilities as stewards of life on this planet. Plus it's going to be a whole lot of fun in the process.

Embracing this shift means venturing beyond our comfort zones. It's about more than adopting new construction techniques; it's about fostering a deeper connection with our very nature and consciousness.

About the author:

Stacey Murphy is a Regenerative Design Expert, an award-winning serial entrepreneur, impact investor, architect, engineer, and the Founder of Dreaming Earth, an architectural venture capital studio with the Earthshot of growing buildings by 2030.

Stacey incubates startups focused on regenerative materials and systems in architecture and construction innovation. Her mission is to accelerate the building blocks of bio-centric cities.

Her experience starting BK Farmyards, a decentralized urban farming network in Brooklyn, led her to consult corporations in Regenerative Design Thinking to improve efficiencies.

Stacey has been featured in Fast Company, New York Magazine, New York Times, BBC, Good, Martha Stewart Radio, David Letterman, PBS, and two TEDx talks on the future of food. You can find her at Stacey.earth

CHAPTER 12
A DUALISTIC PRESENTATION OF THE IMMUNE SYSTEM

Captn Hans Smith

The disruptor hates to be disrupted as much as the manipulator hates to be manipulated, but that is how life works, and is something many realize as they live their life.

Sustainability should be a goal for all individuals and organizations, but our world leaders make it difficult to take seriously. It reflects a failure of the intelligent societies of nations when we are experiencing multiple wars and conflicts today. War is the least sustainable activity for nations, alliances, and regions. Instead, we should prioritize peace and mutual understanding to achieve a prosperous and abundant future. Therefore, sustainability efforts on a personal level seem insignificant while wars are raging – PEACE FIRST!

Two stories inspired by Captain Smith of the Titanic and the concept of the corporate immune system.

Exponential Organizations in Action

Once upon a time, there was a company called Titanic Inc.. It was a massive corporation that had been around for decades and had a reputation for being unsinkable. The company was led by a captain named Edward Smith, who was known for his calm demeanor and his ability to navigate through even the roughest of storms.

One day, a storm hit the company, and it was unlike anything they had ever seen before. The storm was so fierce that it threatened to sink the entire company. But Captain Smith was determined to keep the company afloat, and he rallied his crew to help him.

Together, they worked tirelessly to repair the damage caused by the storm. They patched up holes, bailed out water, and did everything they could to keep the company from sinking. As they worked, they realized that the company had a built-in immune system that was helping them fight off the storm.

The corporate immune system was made up of all the employees who were dedicated to keeping the company running smoothly. They were the ones who worked behind the scenes to make sure that everything was running smoothly, and they were the ones who stepped up when the company was in trouble.

Thanks to the corporate immune system, Titanic Inc. was able to weather the storm and emerge stronger than ever. And Captain Smith knew that he could always count on his crew to help him navigate through any storm that came their way.

The end?

Now the second story where the immune system is an obstacle

Once upon a time, there was a company called Titanic Inc. It was a massive corporation that had been around for decades and had a reputation for being unsinkable. The company was led by a captain named Edward Smith, who was known for his calm demeanor and his ability to navigate through even the roughest of storms.

One day, a storm hit the company, and it was unlike anything they had ever seen before. The storm was so fierce that it threatened to sink the entire company. But Captain Smith was determined to keep the company afloat, and he rallied his crew to help him.

Together, they worked tirelessly to repair the damage caused by the storm. They patched up holes, bailed out water, and did everything they could to keep the company from sinking. But as they worked, they realized that the company had a built-in immune system that was hindering them from adapting to the changing environment.

The corporate immune system was made up of all the employees who were loyal to the company's old ways of doing things. They were the ones who resisted any change or innovation, and they were the ones who sabotaged any new ideas or initiatives. They preferred to stick to the familiar and comfortable, even if it meant risking the company's future.

Because of the corporate immune system, Titanic Inc. was unable to find new and exponential ways of going forward. They missed out on opportunities, lost customers, and fell behind their competitors. Captain Smith realized that he could no longer rely on his crew to help him navigate through any storm that came their way.

The end?

This story is inspired by the tragic sinking of the world's largest, fastest, and what was designed to be an unsinkable ship. This story was a fictional analogy based on the real-life sinking of the Titanic in 1912. The captain of the Titanic was named Edward Smith, and he faced a similar dilemma when his ship hit an iceberg and began to sink.

Captain Smith's actions during the final hours of the Titanic are not very clear. Some witnesses said he was calm and composed, while others said he was shocked and confused. Some said he gave clear orders and helped with the evacuation, while others said he was absent or ineffective. Some said he died heroically on the bridge or in the water, while others said he committed suicide or escaped with a disguise.

The truth is, we may never know for sure what Captain Smith did or why he did it. He was a respected and experienced sailor, but he was also a human being who faced an unprecedented and tragic situation. He may have made mistakes, but he may have also done his best under the circumstances. He may have been a victim of his pride, or he may have been a scapegoat for the failures of others. He may have been a leader, or he may have been a follower.

What do you think? How would you have acted if you were in his position?

What is the corporate immune system?

The corporate immune system is a term used to describe a process within corporations that demands organizations within the company accomplish activities in a certain way, a form of conformity tendency. It is, in effect, the active form of groupthink, when the past outcome of groupthink processes forces itself on organizations that are otherwise different. The corporate immune system is made up of all the employees who are dedicated to keeping the company running smoothly. They are the ones who work behind the scenes to make sure that everything is running smoothly, and they are the ones who step up when the company is in trouble. The term may refer to any organizational process that tends to drive out differences or alternately demands conformity. The name refers to parallels with biological immune systems, which attempt to drive out "foreign" invaders and sometimes react negatively against the organism it is supposed to protect. The corporate immune system can stifle innovation and entrepreneurial activity within organizations, often found in large multi-divisional companies, where it manifests itself as inter-divisional fighting, often subtle or unintended Multinational corporations are particularly common examples, as divisional differences can be compounded by different corporate structures, languages and even time zones.

Photo as an expression/example of abundance - and how the corporate immune system postponed the development of the digital camera;

Peace, Love & Diverstiy
youtube.com/@CaptnSmith
https://www.linkedin.com/in/hsestories/
https://openexo.com/community/hsecaptn

Case Study

Batna (old Norse for Improve) is a company that has a purpose-driven approach. Its purpose is to assist businesses with improving quality, environment, health, and safety in organizations and reputation-enhancing business development.

Founder Hans C Smith, a QHSE leader, consultant, and auditor embodies the mission of "improve & tell." His the journey includes sharing knowledge and methods of improvement with numerous companies and organizations. Driven by interests in peace studies, corporate social responsibility, and sustainability, he also developed a course on sustainability reporting.

This course offers an adaptable, action-focused approach for any company or organization, emphasizing their key products, services, knowledge, and societal context. This perspective persists in the MTP (Massive transformative purpose) MTP - Expanding Economy With HSE stories worth telling in the age of AI & crypto economies Hope, Soul & EnCourage.

Health Safety & Environment

The mission is to inspire companies beyond traditional business metrics, exploring historical perspectives and stories about preventive initiatives. By showcasing how we debunk the fraudulent

foundations of traditional economic theory and how preventive initiatives contribute to economic

expansion through an «improve-and-tell/share" approach. The rational economic choice theory is a contradiction when we see how thriving the the marketing industry is.

Challenging the GDP as a sole measure of growth, we recognize the shift from an industrial to a post-industrial era. While the industrial age had abundant resources, our current reality demands a renewed, more human-oriented economy.

Volunteering and interest organizations struggle with outdated economic models, facing bureaucratic hurdles. The rise of decentralized economies offers hope to disrupt the dysfunctional system and prioritizing what truly matters in life.

Despite resistance from the entrenched "old economy," alternative win-win-win scenarios are plentiful. Breaking free from the antiquated educational systems reveals that there isn't a one-size-fits-all solution. The digital economy can enable diverse, self-reliant economies open to multilateral exchange. Can we find ways to pay for preventive measures and positive actions

Here is an HSE story that hopefully helps in understanding this. If you can go with the premise that the goal of a birthing department is to help deliver healthy babies and dead babies are the opposite of this.

Wash your hands; Ignaz Semmelweis was a Hungarian physician who worked in Vienna General Hospital in the mid-19th century. He noticed that the mortality rate of women giving birth was significantly higher in the ward wheredoctors and medical students worked compared to the ward where midwives worked.

Semmelweis hypothesized that the doctors and medical students were transmitting "cadaverous articles" from the autopsy room to the women in labor, causing them to develop puerperal fever, also known as childbed fever.

To test his hypothesis, Semmelweis ordered his medical students and junior physicians to wash their hands in a chlorinated lime solution before examining women about to deliver babies. The results were remarkable: the mortality rate in the ward where handwashing was implemented

dropped from 18% to 2%. However, Semmelweis's colleagues were skeptical of his hypothesis and refused to accept his findings. They ridiculed him and accused him of being insane.

Semmelweis was eventually dismissed from his position at the hospital and returned to Hungary, where he continued to advocate for handwashing. Unfortunately, he was unable to convince the medical community of the importance of handwashing during his lifetime. It was only after his death that his ideas were accepted and handwashing became a standard medicine practice.

Semmelweis's story is a reminder of the importance of scientific inquiry and the need to challenge established beliefs. His work has saved countless lives and continues to inspire scientists and researchers to this day.

Problem, Not seeing the abundance of possibilities in digital economies and utilizing this, by creating digital currencies with utilization and rewarding preventive actions as a core feature.

Solution Connecting and collaborating with other people, networks, and organizations to create piggyback on existing crypto currency systems.

The Open ExO Framework and Community.

MTP - Expanding Economy With HSE stories worth telling in the age of AI & crypto economies

Hope, Soul & EnCourage Hope

- abundance perspective Soul
- Find your purpose(s) Courage
- to enhance your talent(s) and follow your purpose(s)
- Encourage others to follow their(s) purpose!

Diversity is key!

ExO Attributes/Methodology & the Immune System

A dualistic presentation of the Immune System

The disruptor hates to be disrupted as much as the manipulator hates to be manipulated, but that is how life works, and is something many realize as they live their life.

Two stories inspired by Captain Smith of the Titanic and the concept of the corporate immune system.

Once upon a time, there was a company called Titanic Inc.. It was a massive corporation that had been around for decades and had a reputation for being unsinkable. The company was led by a captain named Edward Smith, who was known for his calm demeanor and his ability to navigate through even the roughest of storms.

One day, a storm hit the company, and it was unlike anything they had ever seen before. The storm was so fierce that it threatened to sink the entire company. But Captain Smith was determined to keep the company afloat, and he rallied his crew to help him. Together, they worked tirelessly to repair the damage caused by the storm.

They patched up holes, bailed out water, and did everything they could to keep the company from sinking. As they worked, they realized that the company had a built-in immune system that was helping them fight off the storm.

The corporate immune system was made up of all the employees who were dedicated to keeping the company running smoothly. They were the ones who worked behind the scenes to make sure that everything was running smoothly, and they were the ones who stepped up when the company was in trouble.

Thanks to the corporate immune system, Titanic Inc. was able to weather the storm and emerge stronger than ever. Captain Smith knew that he could always count on his crew to help him navigate through any storm that came their way.

The end?

Here is the second story where the immune system is an obstacle!

Once upon a time, there was a company called Titanic Inc. It was a massive corporation that had been around for decades and had a reputation for being unsinkable. The company was led by a captain named Edward Smith, who was known for his calm demeanor and his ability to navigate through even the roughest of storms.

One day, a storm hit the company, and it was unlike anything they had ever seen before.

The storm was so fierce that it threatened to sink the entire company. But Captain Smith was determined to keep the company afloat, and he rallied his crew to help him. Together, they worked tirelessly to repair the damage caused by the storm.

They patched up holes, bailed out water, and did everything they could to keep the company from sinking.

But as they worked, they realized that the company had a built-in immune system that was hindering them from adapting to the changing environment. The corporate immune system was made up of all the employees who were loyal to the company's old ways of doing things. They were the ones who resisted any change or innovation, and they were the ones who sabotaged any new ideas or initiatives. They preferred to stick to the familiar and comfortable, even if it meant risking the company's future.

Because of the corporate immune system, Titanic Inc. was unable to find new and exponential ways of going forward. They missed out on opportunities, lost customers, and fell behind their competitors. Captain Smith realized that he could no longer rely on his crew to help him navigate through any storm that came their way.

The end?

This story is inspired by the tragic sinking of the world's largest, fastest, and what was designed to be an unsinkable ship. This story was a fictional analogy based on the real-life sinking of the Titanic in 1912.

The end?

The captain of the Titanic was also named Edward Smith, and he faced a similar dilemma when his ship hit an iceberg and began to sink.

Captain Smith's actions during the final hours of the Titanic are not very clear. Some witnesses said he was calm and composed, while others said he was shocked and confused.

Some said he gave clear orders and helped with the evacuation, while others said he was absent or ineffective.

Some said he died heroically on the bridge or in the water, while others said he committed suicide or escaped with a disguise.

The truth is, we may never know for sure what Captain Smith did or why he did it. He was a respected and experienced sailor, but he was also a human being who faced an unprecedented and tragic situation. He may have made mistakes, but he may have also done his best under the circumstances. He may have been a victim of his pride, or he may have been a scapegoat for the

failures of others. He may have been a leader, or he may have been a follower.

What do you think? How would you have acted if you were in his position?

What is the corporate immune system?

The corporate immune system is a term used to describe a process within corporations that demands organizations within the company accomplish activities in a certain way, a form of conformity tendency. It is, in effect, the active form of groupthink, when the past outcome of groupthink processes forces itself on organizations that are otherwise different. The corporate immune system is made up of all the employees who are dedicated tokeeping the company running smoothly. They are the ones who work behind the scenes to make sure that everything is running smoothly, and they are the ones who step up when the company is in trouble. The term may refer to any organizational process that tends to drive out differences or alternately demands conformity. The name refers to parallels with biological immune systems, which attempt to drive out "foreign" invaders and sometimes react negatively against the organism it is supposed to protect.

The corporate immune system can stifle innovation and entrepreneurial activity within organizations, often found in large multi-divisional companies, where it manifests itself as inter-divisional fighting, often subtle or unintended. Multinational corporations are particularly common

examples, as divisional differences can be compounded by different corporate structures, languages, and even time zones.

The ExO model has a solution to deal with the immune system not stopping disruptive innovations. If the initiative /innovation is disruptive for your business/organization you should create a small group and run it as an edge initiative that is decoupled from the mother organization so that you circumpass the immune system and only have to challenge the limiting beliefs that may still be there. This again depends on how embedded the immune system is in the organizational culture and the individuals it is created by.

In this age of endless innovations, how is your organization tackling the continuous changes? Seeing and learning from history and stories is one element, but utilizing a method like the ExO framework will help you see opportunities and utilize the changes instead of being disrupted by them.

Batna has the knowledge and the network to assist you.

https://insight.openexo.com/leveraging-exponential-organizations-for-iso-success/

Photo as an expression/example of abundance - and how the corporate immune system postponed the development of the digital camera;

https://www.linkedin.com/feed/update/urn:li:activity:7133015935497515008

Peace, Love & Diversity
youtube.com/@CaptnSmith

EPILOGUE:
IGNITING THE EXPONENTIAL AWAKENING

As we close the final chapter of this journey through the landscape of Exponential Organizations, we find ourselves standing at the precipice of a new era—one that we've come to call the Sophia Century, or perhaps more aptly, the Exponential Awakening.

This term, "Exponential Awakening," encapsulates the profound shift in consciousness and capability that exponential thinking brings. It's not about reviving old ideas, but about birthing entirely new paradigms—creating Gutenberg moments that fundamentally alter the course of human progress.

Throughout these pages, we've explored the transformative power of exponential thinking and its practical applications across diverse sectors. From the fundamental principles of ExOs to their implementation in healthcare, finance, architecture, and beyond, we've witnessed the incredible potential of this approach to reshape our world in ways we're only beginning to imagine.

We've seen how small and medium enterprises can leverage ExO principles to compete on a global scale, not by following old rules, but by writing entirely new ones. We've explored the future of health, where personalized medicine and AI-driven diagnostics promise to revolutionize patient care in ways that were science fiction mere decades ago. We've delved into the world of decentralized finance, where blockchain technology is not just democratizing access to financial services, but reimagining the very concept of value exchange.

But perhaps most importantly, we've discovered the power of collective intelligence—the catalyst of the Exponential Awakening. From the innovative un-conference model of GEC4 to the collaborative problem-solving approaches employed by ExO communities worldwide, it's clear that our greatest breakthroughs lie not in individual genius, but in our ability to connect, collaborate, and co-create at unprecedented scales.

As we face global challenges of a magnitude never before seen—climate change, social inequality, technological disruption—the principles and strategies outlined in this book offer more than just incremental improvements. They provide a launchpad for quantum leaps in human capability and planetary stewardship.

The Exponential Awakening is not a distant future scenario. It's unfolding now, with every decision to embrace exponential thinking, to collaborate across boundaries, and to dare to imagine what's never been done before.

To you, the reader, we offer both a challenge and an invitation. The challenge is to take these ideas beyond these pages and into your organizations, your communities, your daily lives—not just to apply them, but to evolve them. The invitation is to join a growing global community of awakened thinkers and doers, committed to shaping a future that surpasses our current capacity to envision it.

Remember, in the Exponential Awakening, the future is not something we predict—it's something we invent. And with the tools of exponential thinking at our disposal, we have the power to invent a future beyond our wildest dreams.

As you close this book, know that your journey is just beginning. The Exponential Awakening is here, and you are its catalyst. Together, let's create a world where wisdom, collaboration, and exponential growth converge to solve our greatest challenges and unlock potentials we have yet to imagine.

The future is exponential. The future is collaborative. The future is now unfolding in ways we never thought possible.

Welcome to the Exponential Awakening. Let's ignite the future.

GLOSSARY

Abundance Thinking – the mindset that recognizes the limitless possibilities and opportunities available in the world, driven by technological advancements that transform scarcity into abundance. For example, the rise of online education platforms has made quality learning accessible to anyone with an internet connection, empowering individuals globally regardless of their socioeconomic status.

Algorithms – systematic procedures or formulas used to solve problems or perform tasks, often by processing data to derive insights or make decisions. For instance, recommendation algorithms on streaming platforms analyze user behavior to suggest personalized content, enhancing user engagement and satisfaction.

Autonomy – the ability of individuals or teams within an organization to operate independently, make decisions, and pursue their objectives aligned with the company's overarching goals. For example, a software development team may be granted autonomy to choose their tools and methodologies, fostering innovation and faster delivery of products while remaining focused on the company's mission.

Awake Process – the essential first phase in the ExO Sprint that fosters stakeholder awareness of the urgent need for transformation due to industry disruption and the potential of exponential technologies. This phase often includes expert-led discussions on emerging trends, enabling organizations to identify significant problems and innovative solutions, ultimately positioning them for future growth and success.

Community & Crowd – Community refers to a dedicated group of individuals who share a strong emotional connection to an organization's Massive Transformational Purpose (MTP) and actively contribute to its goals, often forming lasting relationships and loyalty. For example, the community of Tesla enthusiasts not only advocates for electric vehicles but also engages in discussions and initiatives that support Tesla's mission. Crowd, on the other hand, consists of a broader audience who may not have a direct relationship with the organization but can be incentivized to participate in specific tasks or initiatives, often for transactional rewards. An example of this is crowdsourcing platforms like Kickstarter, where diverse individuals contribute funds to support new projects in exchange for early access or exclusive products.

Dashboards – visual interfaces that consolidate and display real-time data and key performance indicators, enabling organizations to monitor operations and make informed decisions efficiently. For instance, a sales dashboard might showcase metrics like revenue, conversion rates, and customer engagement, allowing teams to quickly identify trends and adjust strategies accordingly.

Disruption (in the context of ExOs) – refers to the transformative impact of innovative technologies or business models that fundamentally reshape markets or industries, often leading to the obsolescence of traditional practices. This process is characterized by the rapid scaling of solutions that address significant global problems, as exemplified by ride-sharing platforms like Uber, which leveraged mobile technology and a peer-to-peer model to disrupt the taxi industry and alter consumer behavior.

Edge Organizations – refers to a decentralized structure that operates at the periphery of traditional organizational boundaries, leveraging external resources, expertise, and networks to drive innovation and adaptability. For example, a tech startup might form partnerships with freelance developers and researchers around the world, enabling it to rapidly prototype and iterate on new products without the constraints of a conventional hierarchical setup.

Engagement – involves employing strategies such as gamification, incentives, and community-driven initiatives to foster active participation and commitment among stakeholders towards an organization's Massive Transformational Purpose (MTP). For instance, Starbucks uses a rewards program that not only incentivizes purchases but also builds a loyal community of coffee enthusiasts who feel a connection to the brand's mission of sustainability and quality.

ExO – stands for exponential organization, a new breed of organization that leverages innovative technologies and flexible structures to achieve tenfold growth and impact compared to traditional companies. For instance, companies like Airbnb and SpaceX exemplify ExOs by utilizing scalable platforms and cutting-edge technologies to disrupt industries and create significant value rapidly.

ExO Sprint – a structured 10-week methodology designed to help organizations innovate and adapt to disruption by leveraging exponential technologies and the ExO Attributes, while simultaneously fostering new initiatives on the edge. For example, a company could use the ExO Sprint to develop a new digital product line that addresses emerging customer needs, while also refining its core operations to stay competitive in a rapidly changing market.

ExQ (Exponential Quotient) - a metric that evaluates an organization's capability to scale rapidly and adapt to change, based on a comprehensive assessment of its exponential attributes through a 21-question survey. For instance, a startup with a high ExQ might effectively leverage emerging technologies and innovative business models, enabling it to achieve significant growth and market impact, similar to companies like Airbnb or SpaceX.

Experimentation – the iterative process of testing ideas and hypotheses through various methods, such as A/B testing, to drive innovation and optimize solutions based on data-driven insights. For example, a software company might run multiple versions of a feature to determine which one enhances user engagement the most, continuously refining their approach based on real-time feedback and results.

Exponential Awakening – the transformative process through which individuals and organizations recognize and embrace the potential of exponential technologies and mindsets to drive significant change and innovation. For instance, a traditional manufacturing company might undergo exponential awakening by adopting 3D printing and IoT technologies, fundamentally reshaping its production processes and business model to enhance efficiency and responsiveness to market demands.

Exponential Canvas – a strategic tool that visually outlines the key components of an Exponential Organization, focusing on elements such as the Massive Transformative Purpose (MTP), SCALE and IDEAS attributes, and information streams. For example, a tech startup might use the Exponential Canvas to map out how its MTP of "empowering global connectivity" aligns with its innovative use of artificial intelligence and community-driven development to achieve rapid growth and impact.

Exponential Mindset – the cognitive framework that enables individuals and organizations to embrace rapid technological advancements and adapt to a fast-changing environment, fostering innovation and resilience. For instance, a leader with an exponential mindset might proactively invest in AI and automation, recognizing their potential to revolutionize business operations and create new market opportunities, rather than clinging to traditional methods.

Exponential Organization (ExO) – refers to a new breed of organization that leverages exponential technologies and innovative business models to achieve tenfold growth and impact compared to traditional organizations. For example, companies like Airbnb and Uber exemplify ExOs by utilizing digital platforms to disrupt established industries, dramatically scaling their operations and market reach with minimal physical infrastructure

Exponential Technologies – advanced innovations that experience rapid growth and performance improvements, often following the patterns described by Moore's Law, leading to disruptive changes across industries. Examples include artificial intelligence, blockchain, and biotechnology, which are revolutionizing sectors like finance, healthcare, and logistics by enabling unprecedented capabilities and efficiencies.

IDEAS (acronym for ExO attributes) – a set of inward-facing attributes that facilitate the control framework and cultural dynamics of an Exponential Organization, encompassing Interfaces, Dashboards, Experimentation, Autonomy, and Social Technologies. For instance, a company might implement Dashboards to provide real-time performance metrics, empowering teams to make data-driven decisions and fostering a culture of continuous improvement and innovation.

Information Enabling – refers to the process of leveraging data and digital tools to enhance decision-making, operational efficiency, and customer engagement within an organization. For example, a retail company might use data analytics to track customer preferences and optimize inventory management, thereby improving sales and reducing waste.

Interfaces – automated processes that facilitate the connection and interaction between different user groups within an Exponential Organization, enabling efficient filtering and matching of resources and information. For example, platforms like eBay and Google AdWords utilize sophisticated Interfaces to streamline user engagement and transactions, allowing both buyers and sellers to operate with minimal friction and maximum scalability.

Iridium Moment – a pivotal point in an organization's journey when it undergoes a transformative change, often triggered by a breakthrough insight or a disruptive innovation that propels it to exponential growth. For example, when Netflix transitioned from DVD rentals to streaming services, it marked an Iridium Moment that fundamentally reshaped its business model and the entire entertainment industry.

Leveraged Assets – resources that an organization utilizes without owning, allowing it to access capabilities or infrastructure on demand, thereby reducing costs and increasing flexibility. For instance, a startup might use cloud computing services like AWS to host its applications, enabling rapid scaling without the burden of maintaining physical servers.

Linear vs. Exponential Growth – Linear Growth refers to a consistent, incremental increase in output or performance over time, where doubling the input results in a proportional doubling of the output, such as a company growing its revenue by 10% year over year. In contrast, Exponential Growth describes a rapid increase where the output accelerates over time, often doubling at regular intervals, exemplified by technologies like smartphones, which saw user adoption grow from millions to billions in just a few years.

Massive Transformative Purpose (MTP) – the overarching, aspirational goal of an organization that drives its mission and inspires a community to work towards significant change, often addressing a fundamental global challenge. For example, SpaceX's MTP is to "Make life multiplanetary," which fuels innovation and attracts a passionate following dedicated to advancing space exploration.

SCALE (acronym for ExO attributes) – the set of attributes that enable an organization to achieve exponential growth by leveraging technology and innovative practices to maximize efficiency and impact. For instance, a company like Airbnb utilizes SCALE by harnessing user-generated content and a global network of hosts to rapidly expand its marketplace without significant capital investment.

Singularity – refers to a hypothetical point in the future when technological growth becomes uncontrollable and irreversible, resulting in profound changes to human civilization, often characterized by the emergence of superintelligent AI. For example, the concept suggests that once AI surpasses human intelligence, it could lead to rapid advancements beyond our current understanding, potentially transforming industries and society in ways we cannot predict.

Social Technologies – digital tools that facilitate collaborative interactions and communication among individuals within an organization, enhancing teamwork and productivity. Examples include platforms like Slack for messaging, Zoom for video conferencing, and Notion for project management, which enable seamless sharing of ideas and resources in real-time.

Sophia Century – an age where human wisdom guides our choices and actions for the benefit of all life on Earth. It's a time of conscious collaboration, where we use our collective intelligence to create a thriving, just, and sustainable world for generations to come.

Staff on Demand (SoD) – refers to the practice of leveraging a flexible workforce of prequalified individuals who can be engaged as needed to fulfill various operational tasks within a business. For example, companies like Uber utilize SoD by tapping into a network of drivers who can be activated on-demand, allowing for scalable operations without the overhead of a permanent workforce.

SWARM – leverages the collective intelligence and diverse skills of participants, often leading to innovative solutions and rapid responses to challenges. The approach is characterized by flexibility, adaptability, and the ability to harness the power of the crowd.

Un-conference Model – a participant-driven meeting format that encourages open dialogue and collaboration, allowing attendees to propose topics and lead discussions rather than following a predetermined agenda. For example, in an un-conference setting, participants might gather to share insights on emerging technologies, with sessions evolving organically based on the interests and expertise of those present, fostering a more dynamic and engaging learning environment.

VUCA – stands for Volatility, Uncertainty, Complexity, and Ambiguity, describing the challenging and unpredictable nature of today's business environment. For example, during the COVID-19 pandemic, companies faced VUCA conditions as they navigated sudden market changes, supply chain disruptions, and shifting consumer behaviors, requiring agile strategies and adaptive leadership.

Made in the USA
Middletown, DE
06 November 2024